Jeffrey Dahmer

Margaret Simpson

Published by Trellis Publishing, 2021.

While every precaution has been taken in the preparation of this book, the publisher assumes no responsibility for errors or omissions, or for damages resulting from the use of the information contained herein.

JEFFREY DAHMER

First edition. July 3, 2021.

Copyright © 2021 Margaret Simpson.

ISBN: 979-8224912117

Written by Margaret Simpson.

Jeffrey Dahmer

Margaret Simpson

Jeffrey Dahmer

Jeffrey Dahmer, also known as "The Milwaukee Cannibal", is infamous for raping, murdering, dismembering, engaging in necrophilia with, and eating parts of at least 17 males, most of them in their teens and early 20s. Despite claiming insanity, Dahmer was convicted of the murders and sentenced to 15 consecutive life sentences in Wisconsin on 15 February 1992, for a total of 957 years, as well as receiving another life sentence in Ohio in May 1992. He was ultimately murdered in prison on 28 November 1994 by convicted killer Christopher Scarver who bludgeoned both Dahmer and another convicted murderer, Jesse Anderson, to death as they were cleaning the prison gymnasium's bathroom. Scarver stated that he was "disgusted" after learning of Dahmer's crimes. Dahmer died en route to the hospital. Scarver received two additional life sentences for the murders.

Early Life

Jeffrey Lionel Dahmer was born on 21 May 1960 in West Allis, Wisconsin—a suburb of Milwaukee—to Lionel Dahmer, a chemist, and Joyce (née Flint). The Dahmers had another son, David, seven years later, who Jeffrey named. According to Lionel, Jeffrey was a happy and curious child who was outgoing and had friends. When Jeffrey was four years old, his father swept some dead animals out from under the house and the small boy took an odd interest in the sounds their little bones made as "his small hands dug deep into the pile"; something that would haunt Lionel for the rest of the life. He would always wonder if it was some omen he should have taken more seriously.

When Jeffrey was six he was diagnosed with a double hernia and required surgery. His father said that his young son never regained his buoyance and exuberance after that, instead, seeming smaller and more vulnerable. When Jeffrey was eight the family moved to Bath, Ohio. His demeanor changed even more and he became shy with an inferiority complex. To help with his adjustment, Jeffrey's parents got him a dog, Frisky, that he loved and cared for.

Having a father who was a workaholic and a mother who wasn't "all there", young Jeffrey did not get much attention and, therefore, had an active imaginary life and very few friends who he tended to scare away. When he was ten, his mother was hospitalized and treated for anxiety. This had an increasingly deleterious effect upon his parents' marriage.

Between the ages of ten and 15, Jeffrey became increasingly withdrawn and uncommunicative and had little interest in social interactions or hobbies. Instead, he would ride his bike around his neighborhood fulfilling his fetish for dead animals which he dissected either in his house or in the woods near his home. One time, he put a dog's head on a stake behind his house. He also enjoyed boiling, or destroying with acid, road kill down to the bones for his own collection. His father stated that during these years his posture changed as well and he became "strangely rigid and inflexible."

Additionally, Jeffrey's budding sexuality and his own realization that he was attracted to men was disturbing to him; however, even more worrisome were Jeffrey's fantasies about murdering and dismembering potential lovers, as well as lying next to an unconscious man. His father attributed this strange behavior to puberty and recollects that his son's interest in seeing the inside of animals was likely the point when everything started going south.

As a student at Revere High School, Jeffrey began drinking heavily to bury his troubling fantasies and to avoid his parents' constant, overt fighting, and, by the time he graduated was a full-blown alcoholic. While in school, however, Jeffrey was a model student who was well-dressed, polite, respectful, and who did his work. Despite having a superior intellect if Jeffrey had no interest in a subject, he would rapidly lose interest and his grades were not as good as they could have been.

Jeffrey's parents divorced shortly after he graduated high school on 4 June 1978, with his father moving into a local motel for a short time and his mother taking his younger brother to Wisconsin with her. Jeffrey was left alone and that neither of them really wanted him had an even more deleterious effect on his psyche. His father remarried shortly before Christmas that year.

Jeffrey "attended" The Ohio State University for one quarter but dropped out because he failed to attend the majority of his classes, preferring, instead, to drink. Consequently, his father urged him to enlist in the Army at the end of 1978. He was stationed in Germany. At first, he did fairly well but was discharged after two years in March 1981, due to his alcoholism. Not wanting to go back to Ohio and face his father, Jeffrey went to Miami Beach, Florida, to enjoy the warm weather. After a few months he returned home, continued to drink heavily, and was subsequently arrested for drunk and disorderly conduct on 7 October 1981.

In 1982, Jeffrey moved in with his grandmother back in West Allis where he stayed for six years. During this time, he embraced his homosexuality and began to frequent Milwaukee gay bars and bath houses where, on at least four occasions, he took men to private booths and drugged them. One victim had to be hospitalized for a week and Jeffrey was subsequently banned from many of them.

His behavior became increasingly odder. Once, his grandmother found a fully-dressed male mannequin in her grandson's closet which he had stolen from a store. Another time she discovered a .357 magnum under his bed. If that wasn't enough, she noticed a variety of strange odors emanating from the basement. One time he had found a dead squirrel and chemically dissolved it.

In August 1982, and then again in September 1986, Jeffrey was arrested for indecent exposure; the second time as a result of his flashing two 12-year-old boys named Richard Kohn and John Ostland. He was placed on probation until 9 September 1987. Six days after his probation ended Dahmer began to kill again.

By the summer of 1988, Jeffrey's grandmother had had it with his disturbing behavior, late nights, and the basement smells and asked him to move out. He found an apartment on Milwaukee's west side that was close to his current job at the Ambrosia Chocolate Factory and moved in on 25 September. The following day, Jeffrey was arrested for drugging and sexually molesting a 13-year-old boy and was sentenced to one year in a work release camp and five years' probation. He was subsequently paroled from the camp two months early and he moved into a new apartment.

He then began his murderous rampage that ended in 1991 when he was arrested.

The Crimes

Stephen Hicks, 19

Dahmer committed his first murder in the summer of 1978 when he was 18. His father was away on business and his mother and brother had just moved out after their divorce. Thus Dahmer had the house to himself. Driving home the evening of 18 June 1978, he picked up a hitchhiker, 19-year-old Stephen Mark Hicks, and offered to take him back to his house so they could drink beer and get high. Dahmer planned to have sex with him. However, when Hicks tried to leave, Dahmer hit him in the head with a ten-pound dumbbell and then strangled him to death. Dahmer's rationale for the murder was that Hicks wanted to leave but Dahmer didn't want him to.

Dahmer dragged Hick's body into the crawlspace under the house where it remained for a few days; however, the smell of death and decomposition became too much so Dahmer cut the corpse into pieces, methodically stripped the flesh from the bones, placed the pieces in plastic bags, and then buried the bags in the backyard. Later, due to fear that neighborhood children or animals might dig up Hicks' remains, Dahmer unearthed them and smashed the bones into pieces which were subsequently strewn throughout the woods.

Steven Tuomi, 24

Nine years after his first murder, on 15 September 1987, Dahmer picked up 24-year-old Steven Tuomi at Club 219 and took him to the Ambassador Hotel where he had booked a room for the night. Dahmer stated that his intentions were to drug the man and then have sex with his unconscious body.

Dahmer claims he has no memory of what actually happened in that room except that he got extremely intoxicated. He wasn't sure if they even engaged in any sexual activity but he claims that when he awakened, Tuomi was dead; beaten badly—his chest caved in—and strangled to death. Dahmer also had bruising on his fists and on one forearm.

Dahmer went out and purchased a large suitcase, brought it back to the motel, and stuffed Tuomi's corpse inside of it. He went home to his grandmother's house, in a cab, where he removed Tuomi's arms, legs, and head from his torso, fileted the flesh from the bones, packaged the fleshy parts in plastic bags, pulverized the bones, and set all of Tuomi's remains—except for his severed head—out on the curb with the rest of the day's garbage.

The entire process took approximately two hours.

Dahmer kept his latest victim's head wrapped in a blanket for two weeks, after which he boiled the head in Soilex—an alkali-based industrial detergent—and bleach so he could keep the skull as a masturbatory stimulus. However, the bleaching made the skull too brittle and Dahmer was forced to crush and dispose of that too.

This second murder occurred so many years after the first one that it is considered more like another "first" murder and not yet indicative of a pattern of serial killing. During this time Dahmer spent time learning how to approach men and how to drug them; essentially preparing himself for his subsequent killings.

Dahmer's subsequent murders would be sporadic for the next two years before accelerating rapidly toward the end of 1990 and into 1991.

James (Jamie) Doxtator, 14

On 16 January 1988, Dahmer offered 14-year-old Native American prostitute James Doxtator $50 accompany him home and pose for nude pictures. Doxtator agreed so Dahmer took him to his basement room where they engaged in sexual activity before Dahmer drugged him. Once the boy was asleep, Dahmer strangled him to death. He left the corpse in his basement for a week before disposing of the body much like he did with Tuomi. Also, like Tuomi, Dahmer kept the boy's skull, boiled it, and kept it for a while before pulverizing it.

Richard Guerrero, 25

25-year-old Richard Guerrero had the bad luck to run into Dahmer at a bar called the Phoenix on 24 March 1988. Dahmer offered the broke Guerrero $50 to come back to his place to pose for nude photos and to spend the night with him. Back in his room, Dahmer drugged Guerrero, strangled him with a leather strap, and then had oral sex with the corpse.

Dahmer dismembered Guerrero's body within a day after his murder, again disposing of the remains and retaining the skull for a few months before also being destroyed.

After Guerrero's demise, Dahmer's grandmother began to wonder about the horrendous odors emanating from her basement. Dahmer's father inspected the room and found "a black sticky residue, similar to what acid does to flesh." When he confronted his son about it, Dahmer said that he had been experimenting with animals and his father accepted that explanation; however, his grandmother asked him to move out in the summer of 1988 due to his habit of bringing strange males home late at night and the foul smells from the basement and garage.

Keison Sinthasomphone (survived)

Dahmer found a small one-bedroom apartment and lived there for a short time. Less than a day after he moved in he was in trouble with the police. He had conned a 13-year-old Laotian boy named Keison Sinthasomphone into coming up to his apartment to pose for nude pictures. (Incidentally, Keison was the older brother of Konerak Sinthasomphone who Dahmer would murder three years later.)

Again, Dahmer drugged the boy and this time he sexually molested him; however, the boy escaped and reported what happened to his parents and the police. Dahmer was charged with second-degree sexual assault and "enticing a child for immoral purposes." He spent one night in jail and was released on bail. On 30 January 1989 Dahmer was found guilty of the charges; however, sentencing would not occur for four more months.

Anthony Sears, 26

On 25 March 1989, Dahmer met 26-year-old biracial aspiring model Anthony Sears at La Cage, another Milwaukee gay bar. Instead of taking him home because he thought the police might be watching him after his last run in with them, Dahmer took Sears to his grandmother's house where the two men engaged in oral sex before Dahmer drugged and strangled him.

The following morning, Dahmer placed Sears' corpse in his grandmother's bathtub so he could decapitate it before removing the flesh and pulverizing the bones, and then disposed of the remains in the trash as had become his usual M.O.

Sears was the first victim from whom Dahmer permanently kept trophies because, by his own admission, he found Sears "exceptionally attractive." Dahmer preserved Sears' skull and genitals in acetone and kept them in his work locker. Sears' skull would be recovered from Dahmer's apartment after his arrest in 1991.

On 23 May 1989, Dahmer had his sentencing hearing in front of Judge William Gardner for the sexual assault charges. Despite the district attorney wanting a prison sentence of at least five years,

Dahmer's attorney, Gerald Boyle, argued that Dahmer had a job and that this was a one-time thing. Dahmer himself took the stand and blamed his actions on his alcoholism and his "marvelous performance by a true psychopath" earned Dahmer a sentence of five years' probation and one year on work release. He was also required to register as a sex offender. Two months before his scheduled release from the work camp, Dahmer was paroled—despite a letter of protestation written by Dahmer's own father not to release him until he obtained psychiatric treatment—and his five years' probation began at this point.

Again, Dahmer moved back in with his grandmother until leaving her house for the final time on 14 May 1990 when he moved into the infamous Oxford Apartments at 924 North 25th Street, Apartment 213. Despite being located in a high crime area, the apartment was close to his workplace, was furnished and, with rent only $300 a month, including everything except electricity, was economical.

Ricky Beeks (aka Raymond Smith), 27

On 29 May 1990, Dahmer met 27-year-old at Club 219. Dahmer asked the newcomer Beeks back to his apartment to pose for some photos. Once back at Dahmer's place, Beeks was drugged and then strangled. Dahmer engaged in sex with the corpse; the first one he admitted to, although it wouldn't be the last.

Like his other victims, Dahmer dismembered the body and threw it out with the trash except for Beeks' skull which he kept and painted.

Eddie Smith, 28

On 14 June 1990, Dahmer met 28-year-old Eddie Smith in another gay bar. Akin to his now-typical M.O., Dahmer offered Smith money to pose for pictures. Once back in Dahmer's apartment, Smith was drugged, strangled, dismembered, and his parts were disposed of with the rest of the trash. A failed attempt to dry out the skull in the oven led to its destruction; thus, Dahmer could not add this one to his budding collection. This time, however, Dahmer took pictures of the Smith's in various stages of dismembering.

Ernest Miller, 22

22-year-old dancer Ernest Miller met Dahmer in front of a bookstore and was offered money to come home with Dahmer for sex. After they engaged in sex, Dahmer—instead of strangling Miller—cut his throat, severing his carotid artery, and placed him in the bathtub for his usual dismembering. This time Dahmer chose to keep Miller's entire skeleton which he stored in the bottom drawer of a filing cabinet, complete with painted skull. Dahmer also kept his victim's heart, biceps, and part of his legs in his freezer for later consumption. Dahmer admitted being particularly attracted to Miller's physique.

It was around this time that Dahmer's neighbors began to complain of the foul stench that came from his apartment. Dahmer blamed it on a broken refrigerator and said that he would get it fixed as soon as possible.

David Thomas, 23

Dahmer met 23-year-old David Thomas on 24 September at the Grand Avenue mall and took him back to his apartment with the promise of being compensated for posing nude. Once there, Dahmer decided that Thomas "wasn't his type" and drugged and strangled him before dismembering him. Dahmer filmed the entire process and then took pictures of Thomas' head in various locations around the apartment. Thomas' sister was shown these photos for identification purposes.

Curtis Straughter, 19

On 7 March 1991, Dahmer met 19-year-old aspiring model Curtis Straughter at a bus stop and offered him money to pose for nude photos; an offer which Straughter gladly accepted. Once back at Dahmer's place, Straughter was drugged, handcuffed, and then strangled while performing oral sex on Dahmer.

Like he did with Thomas' corpse, Dahmer took pictures of the dismembering process. This time he decided to keep his victim's skull, hands, and penis.

Errol Lindsey, 19

As if Dahmer's antics were not gruesome enough. 19-year-old Errol Lindsey—whom Dahmer met on 7 April—was the first of Dahmer's victims upon whom he practiced his "drilling technique" that involved his drilling holes into his victim's skull with a power drill and then injecting muriatic acid into the brain; a crude lobotomy with the hopes of creating a "sex zombie". Dahmer admitted that if he had succeeded then he would have stopped killing and this technique was discovered to have been attempted on four of his victims. In one of several post-sentence interviews, Dahmer explained that he didn't want to keep killing people but wanted to do something to keep one of his partners "alive, interactive, but on [his] terms." He said that the disposal process of his victims was exhausting and he often found himself tripping over body parts in the bathtub while showering. Dahmer justified his idea for a sex zombie by alleging that he wasn't a pure necrophiliac but wanted a partner who was alive but in a permanent zombie-like state and prior to this idea, the only way he knew how to keep them compliant was to kill them.

Dahmer retained Lindsey's skull and he was subsequently identified via dental records.

Tony Hughes, 31

On 24 May, Dahmer had met deaf-mute Hughes at Club 219 and offered him $50 to pose for nude photos and watch videos with him back at his apartment. Once there, Hughes was drugged, strangled, and dismembered, with Dahmer adding his skull to his collection.

Konerak Sinthasomphone, 14

On 27 May, Dahmer met 14-year-old Konerak Sinthasomphone—the younger brother of the boy Dahmer assaulted in 1989 and was for which he was convicted—in front of a mall and offered him money to pose for nude pictures. After he took the photos, Dahmer drugged the boy, had sex with him, and used his drilling technique, injecting acid in his brain. Then Dahmer left to purchase some beer.

During this time, Sinthasomphone had awakened and ran, naked and bleeding, into the street. A couple of neighborhood women—Sandra Smith, 18, and her cousin Nicole Childress, also 18—called the police after finding the boy naked, bleeding from the rectum, and disoriented from the drugs Dahmer had given him. To the police he was just a drunk homosexual and Dahmer confirmed their suspicions by saying that they just had a little lovers' quarrel and that yes, Sinthasomphone was an adult. Police were unconcerned as to whether the boy could confirm Dahmer's story and simply returned him to Dahmer without checking either of their identification. If they had, they would have discovered that the boy was a child and that Dahmer was a registered sex offender. Further, the officers smelled a foul odor in Dahmer's apartment but failed to investigate. In fact, this smell was the decaying corpse of Tony Hughes.

As soon as the police were gone, Dahmer strangled the boy, had sex with his corpse, took pictures, and dismembered him; keeping the skull, which he painted.

The police officers were later suspended for giving the boy back to Dahmer and were ultimately fired; however, they appealed their termination and were subsequently reinstated.

Matt Turner, 20

Dahmer traveled to Chicago, Illinois, for Gay Pride Day on 30 June 1991 where he met 20-year-old Matt Turner at the bus station who he talked into returning to Milwaukee with him. Dahmer paid his bus fare and back at Dahmer's place, he drugged him and strangled him with a strap.

Dahmer cut off Turner's head and placed it in a plastic bag in the freezer and put the rest of Turner's body into a 57-gallon barrel of acid he had recently purchased.

Jeremiah Weinberger, 23

Dahmer again went to Chicago for the Fourth of July holiday. On 4 July, he met Jeremiah Weinberger, 23, at a local gay bar. Dahmer asked Weinberger to return to Milwaukee with him and Weinberger's roommate assured him that Dahmer seemed "all right."

Once back in Dahmer's apartment, the two men had sex and Weinberger spent the night. The following day the man indicated that he wanted to go home, Dahmer offered him a farewell drink that was, of course, drugged. Dahmer strangled Weinberger and put his decapitated head in the freezer and his headless body in the bathtub for a week before adding it to the acid barrel.

Dahmer remarked that Weinberger's death was unique in that he died with his eyes open.

Oliver Lacy, 23

On 19 July 1991, Dahmer was fired from his job at the Ambrosia Chocolate Company for bad attendance.

That same day 23-year-old bodybuilder Oliver Lacy met Dahmer on the street and agreed to accompany him back to his apartment after Dahmer offered him money to pose for pictures. Lacy was drugged and strangled with a leather strap. This time, Dahmer embraced his necrophiliac tendencies and sodomized the corpse before dismembering it. He put the head in the refrigerator and the heart into the freezer for later consumption. The flesh went into the acid barrel and Dahmer kept the rest of the skeleton for the private shrine of skulls and skeletons he was in the process of creating.

Joseph Bradehoft, 25

On 16 July, Dahmer met his last victim Joseph Bradehoft, 25, a father of three who was in Milwaukee from Illinois looking for work, at a local bus stop. It was raining and Bradehoft had a six-pack so they returned to Dahmer's apartment "to party". After engaging in oral sex, Dahmer drugged and strangled Bradehoft.

He then kept the body in his bed, sleeping with it at night, for the next few days until the head became infected with maggots. After Dahmer cleaned it, it was placed into the refrigerator and the body went into the 57-gallon barrel of acid.

Arrest and Investigation

32-year-old Tracy Edwards met Dahmer on 22 July 1991, and accompanied him back to his apartment under the pretense of posing for nude photographs for $100, as well as to drink beer and just keep Dahmer company. Upon entering Dahmer's apartment, Edwards noted several boxes of muriatic acid on the floor and smelled a foul odor. When Dahmer told Edwards to look at his tropical fish and the man turned his head, Dahmer was able to place a handcuff upon one of Edwards' wrists. Edwards wouldn't let him cuff his hands together so Dahmer told him to accompany him into the bedroom to pose for pictures.

In Dahmer's bedroom Edwards noticed that a videotape of *The Exorcist III* was playing on the television, in addition to nude male posters on the wall and a 57-gallon drum in the corner with a strong, foul odor emanating from it. Dahmer then brandished a large butcher knife and, in an effort to appease him, Edwards unbuttoned his shirt and said he would agree to whatever Dahmer wanted if he would remove the handcuff and put the knife away.

At this point, Dahmer turned his focus toward the television and Edwards stated in court that he observed Dahmer "rocking back and forth and chanting" while watching the movie. When Dahmer turned his attention back to Edwards he put his head on the man's chest and informed him that he intended to eat his heart.

To prevent Dahmer from hurting him, Edwards pretended to be his friend and told him that he wasn't going to escape even though he had already decided he would jump from a window or run out the unlocked front door at his earliest opportunity.

Edwards asked to use the bathroom and then if they could sit in the living room and drink a beer because there was air conditioning in that room. Dahmer agreed. Edwards then asked, again, to use the bathroom and when he stood and noticed that Dahmer had "zoned out" again and was not holding the handcuffs, he punched Dahmer in the face, kicked him in the abdomen, and ran out through the front door.

At 11:30 p.m., Edwards flagged down two police officers—Robert Rauth and Rolf Mueller—down the street from Dahmer's apartment. The officers asked him about the handcuff and Edwards told them about the "freak" in the apartment down the road. When the officers' handcuff key wouldn't remove the cuff on Edwards' wrist, he agreed to accompany the officers back to the apartment where Edwards told them that he had spent the past five hours before "escaping".

Initially, Dahmer acted friendly toward the officers; however, Edwards told them about the large butcher knife with which he was threatened that was still in the bedroom with other weird stuff. After one officer checked the bedroom and saw—and smelled—what Edwards had, he told his partner to arrest Dahmer.

A subsequent search yielded a human head in the refrigerator, at which time one officer shouted something along the lines of, "Oh my God! There's a fuc*ing head in here!" The head was on the bottom shelf, facing upward in a cardboard box with some blood drippings on the bottom. The calm and compliant Dahmer then turned on the two officers and after a brief struggle he was subdued, handcuffed, and arrested.

A subsequent search of the apartment found plastic bags containing two frozen human hearts and strips of human flesh. In another, smaller, free-standing freezer against the kitchen wall were three more severed heads stored in plastic bags with twist ties, a plastic bag containing a human torso, and another plastic bag stuck to the bottom that contained more human flesh and various internal organs.

In the bedroom closet was a metal stockpot that contained decomposed hands and a penis. On a shelf above the pot were two skulls. Also in the closet were containers of formaldehyde, chloroform, and ethyl alcohol, in addition to glass jars that held male genitals.

A number of graphic Polaroid photographs—74 in all—that Dahmer had taken during various stages of his victims' deaths and dismemberments were found throughout the apartment. Several torsos were found in the acid-filled vat. Inside of a file cabinet in Dahmer's bedroom investigators found three painted skulls atop a black towel and a complete human skeleton in the bottom drawer. Also in the bottom drawer were two paper bags; in one was the dried remains of a human scalp and the other contained dried and mummified male genitals. Finally, a sketch of Dahmer's proposed altar of human skulls and bones. A total of seven skulls were found.

Additional evidence included bloodstains on the walls and mattress; the electric drill and a large hypodermic needle for his drilling technique; several gay pornographic videos; a handsaw; a King James' Bible; Odorsorb and incense; four boxes of muriatic acid; a jug of Chlorox bleach; a claw hammer; and a large knife, the one with which he had threatened Edwards and presumably cut Miller's throat.

On 25 July 1991, Dahmer was charged with four murders and his bail was originally set at $1 million cash only. It was increased to $5 million by 22 August after additional murder charges were added, bringing the total to 15. He was not charged with the attempted murder of Tracy Edwards.

Investigators in Ohio found the remains of Steven Hicks in the backyard of Dahmer's grandmother's house and three days later the state of Ohio charged Dahmer with this murder too.

Trial and Conviction

Against his attorney's advice, Dahmer pled guilty but mentally ill on 13 January 1992 in order to avoid having the trial prove that he did, in fact, commit all the murders. Instead, the totality of gruesome details was to be presented to prove that Dahmer was insane because only a crazy person would do what he did.

On 30 January, Dahmer's trial began in front of Judge Laurence Gram. At trial, two detectives took turns reading Dahmer's 160-page confession. In it, Dahmer said, "It's hard for me to believe that a human being could have done what I've done, but I know that I did it" and he claimed his fear of detection was overwhelmed by his "excitement of being completely in control".

The issue of cannibalism is a salient and oft-cited one when one discusses Jeffrey Dahmer. According to experts, cannibalism is not unusual for necrophiliacs. Dahmer himself claimed that he ate his victims' flesh because he believed that people would come alive again inside of him. He said that he got sexually excited when he did so and also used a variety of seasonings and tenderizers to improve the taste. He also admitted that he did not care for the taste of human blood.

On 15 February the jury delivered its verdict after a five-hour deliberation. In a 10-2 vote, jurors found that Dahmer was, indeed, sane and not suffering from some mental disorder at the time of the 15 murders. On the first two counts, he was sentenced to life plus ten years. The remaining 13 counts carried mandatory life-plus-70-years sentences. Capital punishment was not an option as Wisconsin had abolished the death penalty in 1853.

In sum, Dahmer was sentenced to 15 consecutive life terms for total of 957 years in prison.

Three months after he was convicted of the 15 Milwaukee murders, Dahmer was extradited to Ohio for his trial in the death of Steven Hicks. Dahmer pled guilty in a 45-minute hearing and was sentenced on 1 May 1992 to a 16th life sentence.

Incarceration and Death

During his first year in prison, Dahmer was in administrative segregation—essentially solitary confinement—because prison officials were worried about his physical safety if he were to come in contact with other inmates. Despite being in prison, inmates have their own code of "ethics" and certain offenders, such as child molesters, are reviled and oftentimes injured.

While serving time at the Columbia Correctional Institution in Portage, Wisconsin, Dahmer got baptized and declared himself to be a born-again Christian.

He was attacked twice in prison The first time occurred in July 1994, when an inmate tried to cut Dahmer's throat with a homemade "shank" comprised of a razor blade attached to a toothbrush handle while he was returning from a church service to his cell. He was not hurt badly. However, on 28 November 1994, while he and another convicted murderer, Jesse Anderson, were cleaning the bathroom in the prison gymnasium, they were attacked by another convicted killer, Christopher Scarver—the third man on the cleaning crew—who bludgeoned the two of them with a metal bar taken from a piece of gym equipment. A bloodied broomstick was also found near Dahmer's body. Speculation abounds that Scarver killed him because the majority of Dahmer's victims were black. Dahmer was found by correctional officer face down in a pool of blood with the back of his head bashed in. Dahmer died en route to the hospital from severe head trauma and Anderson died two days later. Scarver received two additional life sentences for the crimes which he said Jesus told him commit.

When Dahmer's mother was informed about her son's death, she was angry, lashing out at the media with, "Now is everybody happy? Now that he's bludgeoned to death, is that good enough for everyone?" His victims' families had mixed responses; however, the majority was, as would be expected, happy that he was gone.

Many ask why does a Jeffrey Dahmer happen? In many cases of serial killers, one looks into their childhoods for some problems such as bad parenting, fetal alcohol syndrome, sexual abuse, head trauma, or drug addiction. Whereas in some cases these could be contributing factors, in Dahmer's case he had a good childhood and his father tried to do everything that he could to make his son more social and participatory. He does point to the family's move from Wisconsin to Ohio as a time of great turmoil in his son's life..

Dr. James Fox, Dean of the College of Criminal Justice at Northeastern University and recognized serial killer expert, called Dahmer unusual in that in most cases, the killer enjoys the control leading up to the murder; however, for Dahmer, the death was just the beginning of his subsequent "fun".

Aftermath

The Oxford Apartments, where so many men met their untimely demise, was demolished in 1992. Originally, a memorial garden was planned for the area but now it is just an empty lot.

Dahmer's father published a book in 1994 entitled *A Father's Story* and donated a portion of the proceeds to the victims' family. Lionel and his second wife, Shari, have retained their surname and state that despite what Jeffrey did, they still love him. Dahmer's mother Joyce died of cancer in 2000 and his brother David changed his last name and now lives in anonymity.

Eleven of his victims' families sued Dahmer for damages. In 1996, attorney Thomas Jacobson, who represented eight of these families, held a planned auction of Dahmer's estate to raise $1 million. This sparked considerable controversy when the Milwaukee Civic Pride civic group was created. The group pledged $407,225 which included $100,000 by Milwaukee real estate tycoon Joseph Zilber to purchase Dahmer's possessions which were subsequently destroyed and "buried in an undisclosed Illinois landfill."

Dahmer has been widely represented in popular media. He was the subject of a 1992 comic book by Hart Fisher entitled *Jeffery [sic] Dahmer: An Unauthorized Biography of a Serial Killer, Collector's Item Issue,* as well as another comic book created by cartoonist John Backderf who attended middle and high school with Dahmer entitled *My Friend Dahmer*. He was featured in the sixth episode of the Discovery Channel's *Most Evil* documentary series, as well as a 2012 documentary entitled *Jeff*. Dahmer provided the basis for Joyce Carol Oates' novel *Zombie* (1995). In films, Dahmer has been portrayed by Carl Crew in 1993, Jeremy Renner in 2002, and Rusty Sneary in 2006.

MANIAC

FRANK COLEMAN

*Stranger than **Fiction***

In 2010, journalist Denis Faye sat down with industry expert Pat Brown in an attempt to bridge the gap between how serial killers are portrayed in film and television and how they are in real life. Brown quickly cuts through the existing information floating around on this disparity.

> *"Faye: So what does Hollywood get right about serial killers?*
> *Brown: Very little."*

In the case of "real life" serial killer Alexander Pichushkin, known as the infamous Bitsa Maniac, the Chessboard Killer, and arguably one of Russia's most consummate serial killer, it's almost impossible to draw the line between fact and fiction. Between his mysterious past, the inventiveness of the press, and his own fabrications, Pichushkin's story requires an eye for the difference between killers from the silver screen and true monsters.

Described as a "real-life criminal profiler," Pat Brown has a lot to say about the difference between the fictional serial killers we see in movies and television and the all too real murderers we catch glimpses of in the news. In an interview with the WGA, she attempted to outline some of the most prominent errors writers make when depicting serial killers. She immediately honed in on the false complexity that writers default to in order to create drama, lamenting that such specificity is almost never the case.

> *"They're not as bizarre as the films show... [They] tend to over-profile the killer's mental state."*

In the news, Alexander Pichushkin's story has been sensationalized and stretched, the gaps in his narrative filled with fiction. Between 1992 and 2006 Pichushkin was responsible for the deaths of up to

62 people, putting him in the running for being one of Russia's most prolific serial killers. But despite this infamy and attention, there are plenty of holes in the account of his killing spree for reporters to expound and invent. Even Pichushkin's Wikipedia entry contains an entirely fictional tale of his childhood inspired solely by his title as the Chessboard Killer. This moniker may be the most popular and certainly most evocative option for Pichushkin, but it is by no means the most accurate. Those who were most affected by this slew of murders and know the most about them, locals and experts alike, all prefer the more succinct and accurate name Pichushkin had earned: the Maniac.

Creating a **Monster**

Psychologists often argue whether the monstrousness of serial killers is born or made by trauma or environment. On one hand, being able to point a finger at exactly what caused a human being to do such horrible things can be comforting, but all too often external factors are used to distance killers from blame and evoke sympathy. Brown laments that this distancing is what she is most opposed to in the portrayal of serial killers. "I've never seen a serial killer with redeeming qualities or one you can have some kind of sympathy for, like it's just a bad hobby he's got." On the other hand, a world with the potential for people who are simply born to commit heinous murders is a scary one to imagine, and given the number of environmental similarities between serial killers, one that frankly doesn't seem to exist.

Currently, the prevailing argument is that it is a combination of the natural and nurtured elements of someone's personality that react upon one another to create a psychopath, though Brown feels there is more of a conscious choice involved. "He's just pissed off at society and became a psychopath when life didn't work out his way..." In the case of Pichushkin, close analysis of his childhood, family, and early social interactions reveal many of the trademarks common in other serial killers, however, Brown's reminder of free will is an important one to keep in mind. While Pichushkin's childhood has some traumatic roots, ultimately he was not *made* into a monster—he *chose* to commit murder, and on a minimum of 52 separate occasions.

On April 9th, 1974 Alexander Pichushkin was born in Mytishchi, Moscow, and according to his mother, Natasha Pichushkina, he was a normal child as far as she could tell. Alexander, or Sasha for short, lived in a modest one bedroom apartment with his father and mother who had grown up in that same apartment. The complex is one of many on the outskirts of Moscow, a decaying remainder of soviet era infrastructure and some of the only reasonably priced housing in the area. Nicknamed *khrushchevki* after Nikita Khrushchev, the spartan public housing lacks charm and personality, but continues to serve in functionality and affordability. A mere nine months after Sasha is born, his father leaves Natasha to raise their son alone.

> *"I tried to raise him like a normal mother... I know now that I raised my son very poorly... [but] I can't say what I did wrong."*

Besides his mother's account in a popular interview from 2007, not much is known about young Sasha's childhood. One of the few verified details of Sasha's childhood is the head trauma he incurred at the age of four when he fell backward off a swing outside the *khrushchevki* only for it to swing toward him again and strike his forehead. Immediately following the incident he spent time in an institution for the disabled, though exactly how long he stayed there is not reported. Brain injuries, specifically to the frontal lobe where Sasha was struck, are very common among serial killers. David Berkowitz, Leonard Lake, Kenneth Bianchi, and John Gacy all suffered similar head trauma early in life, which neuroscientists link to violence and impulse control issues, as well as emotional and empathetic difficulties.

There are plenty of other mixed and unsubstantiated accounts of torment in Sasha's childhood inflicted by bullies instead of by accident, including one anecdote about a group of children ganging up on Sasha to steal his moped. A police investigator offered a possible explanation in an interview, saying that "Pichushkin" is a name with an effeminate, weak connotation, a detail that would otherwise be lost to the cultural barrier. Entrenched in a Russian cultural context often tinged with homophobia and toxic ideas of masculinity, young Sasha had his cards stacked against him. With the effeminate name, an absent father, a stint in an institution, and very few, if any, friends, he was ideal fodder for grade school bullies. Despite Pichushkin eventually outgrowing his childhood weaknesses and becoming a model image of Russian masculinity, many experts speculate that he might not be heterosexual.

Mentioned only briefly in an interview with the lead investigator, the question of the Bitsa Maniac's sexuality was quickly brushed off. Pichushkin smoked and drank, had a menial physical job stocking shelves at a grocery store, and a low voice with a gruff personality—to those surrounded by the cultural context of Russia's now-infamous homophobia, there was no possible way he could be anything but straight. Add in the brutal success of his murderous impulses and there is no hope of swaying the investigation's narrow image of Pichushkin.

His mother Natasha brought up in her 2007 interview that he never seemed to be interested in women or sex in general. His only documented emotional attachment is to a male classmate from his teens. An overwhelming majority of his victims, the people he was able to lure most easily and was most comfortable with, are all male ranging from as young as nine years old to retirement age. While there was never evidence of any sexual assault on his male victims to substantiate any of these claims, there also was a complete lack of sexual activity with his female victims as well. Based on the available, though sparse, information, it seems just as likely that Sasha lacked sexual impulse at all, and instead only had a lust to kill.

Yet another facet in the claims against Pichushkin's heterosexuality, young Sasha seemed to be heavily influenced by another serial killer, Andrei Chikatilo, whom he idolized to the extreme. Chikatilo's crimes came to light just as Sasha reached his most consciously formative years, and he kept careful track of his contemporary's every move. Chikatilo's spree of murders earned him the nickname of the Rostov Ripper, but he, like Sasha, was deemed by the press a maniac.

Finding **Inspiration**

In December of 1991 the newly liberated Russian media received news of an arrest made in relation to the series of unsolved, gruesome murders happening 117 miles northeast of Moscow, in Rostov von don. For nearly a decade the area had been terrorized by murders that were clearly linked to the same killer, who had been referred to as the Rostov Ripper. Immediately after the arrest, sensationalist news sources had yet to learn his name or see his photo, but had a brief summary of his crimes. His signature was stabbing, usually in excess of 30 times, gouging of the eyes, sexual assault, and evisceration; accused of 53 counts of murder in this style, the man whose name would later be learned became simply *the Maniac*. The public did not lay eyes upon the monster that they knew so little about until he appeared at the first day of his trial on April 14th the following year.

Just five days after Sasha's eighteenth birthday the media is suddenly saturated with the face of the Rostov Ripper, now revealed to be Andrei Chikatilo. His sallow face is pictured from behind iron bars throughout the trial, specially put in place of the usual plexiglass box, to protect him from the often hysterical and retaliatory relatives of his victims. These attacks were not the only noteworthy outbursts of the trial: Chikatilo and the judge, Leonid Akubzhanov, remained combative toward each other throughout the proceedings, with Chikatilo refusing to cooperate. Ignoring questions posed by the prosecution, Chikatilo's original well-spoken demeanor devolved into a show-stopping display of chaos, singing socialist anthems and exposing himself to the jury in an attempt to be deemed unfit to stand trial.

As the trial continued into the summer, news outlets revealed more of Chikatilo's gory past, full of sexual assault while in his teaching position, torturous excess during his killings, and the numerous occasions he was apprehended, questioned, or suspected before his final arrest. Sasha followed all of these stories with more than the morbid curiosity typical of a boy his age. He clipped articles from the papers and kept photos of Chikatilo's face, images with captions that described him as a "shaven-skulled demon" and articles detailing the horrific, decade long murder spree of *the Maniac*.

With the clarity of hindsight, Pichushkin's serial murders appear to be somewhat spawned from Chikatilo's, if not directly inspired. Teenaged Sasha was exposed to widespread press coverage of his killings and saw the attention he garnered from the public and his victims' families. He witnessed the controversy over Chikatilo's punishment, which arguably contributed to the suspension of Russia's death penalty in 1996 (notably, after executing yet another serial killer, Sergey Golovkin). At the very least, Pichushkin seemed intent on surpassing Chikatilo in number, keeping track of his alleged 61 victims with numbers pasted on his now-infamous chessboard. While journalists after the fact like to fixate on this chessboard and invent a final goal of filling it with 64 murders, Pichushkin never mentioned the board in his taped confession. Motivated only by his need to kill and desire to overshadow the Rostov Ripper, the lead police investigator doubted Pichushkin would stop when he ran out of squares.

"Pichushkin is quite an unusual serial killer he's a hunter, a typical hunter and his only motivation was to kill, there was no other motive, whatever else we might have thought."

*A New **Maniac** Begins*

On the 27th of July, Sasha takes his first step towards becoming the infamous Bitsa Maniac. Now three months after turning eighteen years old, he invites his friend and classmate Mikhail Odichuck to join him in something he has been ruminating possibly for years: to commit his first murder. For Pichushkin, this is the most intimate gesture he could possibly offer. Only a trusted friend, a confidante, someone he would deem worthy of sharing such a powerful experience of control and subversion of societal expectations could have been welcomed so wholly into Sasha's inner circle. Unfortunately for both boys, what Sasha viewed as a generous offer, Mikhail saw as a joke.

It would be easy to jump to the conclusion that Sasha held some form of fondness or affection towards his classmate Mikhail. With the seeming absence of his sexual attraction to women in combination with idolization of Chikatilo and experience being bullied as a child, their relationship could have even been interpreted as a boyhood crush. Out of 51 charges of murder and attempted murder, only three victims were female, a statistic that belies Pichushkin's gravitation toward men in general. At such an important developmental stage in his life, Sasha would be expected to display sexual and emotional attraction towards those he felt closest to at the time, namely his friend Mikhail. With over a decade of experience in examining the personalities of serial killers, specialist Pat Brown would insist otherwise.

> *"What people don't get is that a psychopath can portray, at certain points in his life, certain levels of affection... [but] those are just objects in his life... People are either useful, or they're in the way."*

Mikhail made the mistake of getting in the way. Eventually the boy realized Sasha was dedicated to the idea of murder—and completely prepared. He knew to prey on the elderly and the homeless, strangers, who wouldn't be missed by family or valued by the police enough to warrant further investigation. He had already crafted the story of his "beloved" dog's grave in Bitsa Park as a trick to lure their victims with promise of a free drink, both lowering their victim's guard and impeding their ability to fight back. Most importantly, Sasha had discovered the manholes in Bitsa Park that fell up to 18 meters deep, full of highly pressurized currents, in which he would later dispose of twenty to thirty bodies. At exactly what point Mikhail came to the realization that Sasha was deadly serious, only Pichushkin knows—but his classmate never made it to the forest. That Monday afternoon Mikhail's lifeless body is found in the street, after dropping from a five-story balcony. Young Sasha was questioned by police, but they never suspected his involvement and ruled the tragedy a suicide with little to no other inquiry.

Prompted by Pichushkin's confession fifteen years later, a follow-up investigation examined Mikhail's body and discovered head trauma that didn't fit within expectations of impact on the ground. What they had glossed over appeared to be evidence that 18 year old Sasha had bashed in his classmate's head up to 21 times with an unidentifiable blunt object before lifting his lifeless body over the edge of the balcony to drop into the street below. Though the final result is similar to the neat, premeditated M.O. he would adopt later in life, this first murder was a crime of passion, fueled by betrayal and rage, and a moment Pichushkin would later look back on fondly.

"This first murder," he began in his televised confession, "It's like first love—It's unforgettable."

An *Experimental Phase*

For the next nine years, Pichushkin waits. Investigators speculated that Sasha repressed his homicidal urges for as long as possible, knowing that he would not be able to stop once he started again. Pichushkin neither confirmed nor denied these claims, and has offered no other explanation for such a long hiatus. But after those nine years are up, Sasha embarks on a personal journey with an astonishing body count, to discover all the ways he can kill and all the ways he can get away with it.

Now at the age of 27, Sasha began to mix up his M.O., experimenting with weapons, victims, and body disposal. The homeless were his first choice of victims, on whom he tested out another toss over the balcony and a homemade "pen shooter" Sasha had crafted himself; Pichushkin lamented in an interview that both of these methods were over too quickly. This second falling victim was only nine years old, whose death was overlooked just like Mikhail's. As for the pen shooter incident, Pichushkin later described the murder in his confession with explicit detail, from finding a homeless man sleeping on the street, to pressing the makeshift gun to his temple in broad daylight and watching him bleed. He explained that he had seen the man as an opportunity while he was walking to work and couldn't resist.

Eventually he moved on to victims who needed to be lured into the cover of the park, but these still would not be the bodies found by police and attributed to the Bitsa Maniac. The story Sasha told many of his victims centered on a "beloved" deceased dog, whose grave, he told them, was in the park. He would offer a drink of vodka over the nonexistent burial site to distract and relax them; little did they know that the spot he lead them to was strategically located by one of the manholes he had discovered in his youth. Sasha would then bash their heads on the manhole cover, only to open it and lift their inebriated or even unconscious bodies over the edge. His story varied slightly each time, and he continued to use opportunities like the sleeping homeless man to take advantage of poor drunks who wouldn't be missed amid his more focused strategy. Yet another distinction between fact and fiction, where news outlets attempted to fit all of Pichushkin's murders into a neat little box, Brown argues that just isn't so.

"[A real serial killer] doesn't have a fantastic signature with every crime, something really creepy that links every one of the crimes together ... It's very exciting, but it's not the way it is in real life. He's not always going to use the same method. He might try something else on another day, so you have to be careful of that."

When he later told police of his use of the sewer system to dispose of the corpses, they tested its validity by dropping a mannequin inside, only for it to be immediately torn apart by the forceful currents. They also later found the body of a missing person whose death Pichushkin had claimed fault of further into the system. Pichushkin blamed the police force's ineptitude for not being able to find the bodies he had so effectively destroyed. Normally the police would have to rely on what little evidence they have to corroborate a murderer's often fantastical claims and any particulars are reliant on the trustworthiness of a murderer. In Pichushkin's case, his haste to kill left three survivors in his wake who told police and the press every minute detail.

The first to live to tell the tale was Maria Viricheva, who was pregnant at the time of her attempted murder. Pichushkin met her in a metro station on February 23rd 2002 and must have been able to recognize that she was in pressing financial need. He crafted a story of cameras he had hidden away in a manhole in Bitsa Park, offering to sell them to her at a discount so she might turn a profit. Desperate, Maria accepted and followed him into the forest. At the opening to the sewer, Maria quickly realized her mistake as Pichushkin grabbed her and beat her head against the lid, which he then opened and dropped her inside. Miraculously, Maria maintained consciousness, and gripped the slippery walls while attempting to regain some strength amidst the freezing currents. Maria estimated that she spent almost 20 hours trapped in the sewer, struggling between trying to find a way to climb out and her fading will to live. Eventually she discovered rungs that lead to another manhole and was able to climb out to safety.

In addition to Maria, 13 year old Mikhail Lobov fell victim to Pichushkin's invitation to the park for a free drink and cigarettes. Mikhail was just one of many in a crowd of leather jackets and piercings, often hanging around the metro stations, loitering in front of food stands, and drinking. Investigators were unable to find any footage of Mikhail and Pichushkin together in the metro station nearest Bitsa Park, but they still speculate that the most likely place they met would be there. Once in the park, Mikhail's story reads like just like the others—an offer of vodka over the imaginary dog's grave, head meets manhole cover, and into the sewer he goes. The exception to the normal script comes when Mikhail's leather jacket catches on a piece of metal rather high up in the sewer, and his fall is stopped before he even reaches the water. Completely unaware, Pichushkin leaves the park thinking he killed the boy. Just moments later, Mikhail is able to crawl out shaken and disturbed, but with only minor head injuries.

Possibly the most unsettling part of these survivors' stories is when they turn to the local police to report their attacker, only to be turned away. Hospitalized and having just received news that she lost her pregnancy, Maria Viricheva frantically described the entire ordeal from beginning to end, including a full description of Pichushkin's appearance. Instead of taking action, police ignored her account and instead asked for her citizenship documentation. Maria didn't have any, and the police generously offerto ignore the whole situation, leaving her injured and alone in a hospital with Pichushkin continuing his murder spree.

When Mikhail went to police, they brushed him off as a lying punk and told him to go home. Not a month later, Mikhail ran into Pichushkin in a crowded metro station and began yelling and pulling at his hair in frustration, dragging his attacker over to a policeman standing guard and demanding vindication. The officer escorted

Mikhail out of the station and told him again just to go home. Possibly even worse is the third survivor case, of a middle aged homeless man whose story has continued to be ignored and undocumented, even in the wake of Pichushkin's conviction.

Corroborated by these detailed survivor accounts, Pichushkin's confession weaves in the rest of the story. While the sewer was serving him well for body disposal, he still wasn't getting the satisfaction he was looking for. Instead of simply using the manhole cover, Sasha escalated to bringing a yellow-handled utility hammer with him to bash in the skulls of his victims before throwing them in the sewer. At this point, around thirty people had gone missing from his neighborhood. Police still weren't interested in the goings-on of the lower class, but the local gossip had begun to gain footing and Sasha wanted credit for his work.

The Hunt for the **Bitsa Maniac**

It's not until August 15th, 2005 that the police discover their first body, deep in Bittsevsky Park. The victim was a 31 year old man named Nikolai Wirogiev, who had suffered extensive head trauma and, most shockingly, had a vodka bottle lodged in the wound. Law enforcement officer Denis Adamenko was one of the first on the scene; years later he is still able to pinpoint the exact place the first body was found, and describe the scene with gruesome detail. Though he had no idea what was in store at the time of the first police-documented murder, Adamenko would continue working on the case from the first body to Pichushkin's trial.

One month later, another man with the same injuries is found in the park. Just two weeks after that yet another body is found, and then again after only one week. Very suddenly the police began to link the murders together, realizing these stranger killings had to be the handiwork of a single killer. Though the vodka bottle signature isn't present every time, bodies begin piling up within the same age range and sex, all with substantial brain injuries. Sometimes in lieu of a vodka bottle, sticks are found in the wounds, but the reasoning for their presence remains the same: Sasha now likes to play with his victims after the fact.

Brown's interview offers some further insight into Pichushkin's newest escalation, explaining that the often-overlooked element of power is usually what creates specific signatures, such as the vodka bottle or sticks, instead of overly complex motives. "It's just that the fun ends too quickly, so instead of walking away from the body, they want to play with it because they can continue having control. *Now I'm eating you! Look at that!* It's an ongoing feeling of power."

In November of 2005 the police receive a wake up call in the form of the brutalized body and fifth victim of the unknown serial killer, a man named Nikolai Zakharchenko who was a 63 year old pensioner and an ex-cop. Like many of Pichushkin's victims, Zakharchenko lived in the same *khrushchevki* with his family, just two doors down from his murderer. Up until this point, every victim had been part of the underprivileged lower class, either homeless without family or deemed low priority by biased police. Claiming Pichushkin consciously targeted members of society that would not be missed or investigated, as some news sources allege, would be giving him far too much credit. An opportunist at heart, Sasha simply killed whenever he had the chance, with no regard for background or lack thereof, leading to the critical mistake of killing the former policeman. It's only at this point that police give the case with an accumulating body count over to an elite murder squad within the force. What the investigators don't know is that the fifth body that they've found is actually the 41st murder Sasha would later be convicted of.

By the beginning of the next year, news of a serial killer in Moscow had been upgraded from rumors among the working class to front page news. Reports from the Moscow Times warned residents of murders in

Bittsevsky Park, introducing the nickname 'Bitsa Maniac' for the first time. Pichushkin's half sister Katya, who lived in the same apartment as Sasha with her husband and child, later discussed in an interview seeing a news reel about the Maniac on tv and panicking for her brother's safety. It was well known that Sasha frequented the park, but she recalls he was never afraid that there was a killer on the loose. Meanwhile, the body count continued to rise.

A **Red Herring** in Bitsa Park

In a fit of desperation, both the police and the general public began speculating wildly about the killer's possible identity. The investigation's gaze soon turned to the sanitarium looming suggestively on the edge of Bitsa Park. Many of the patients at the ward had privileges that included the freedom to leave the building during the day without aid, and police could not help but notice that the dumping grounds fell well within walking distance. Officers immediately restricted this freedom pending further inquiry; what began as a series of interviews eventually escalated into the interrogation of every single patient with the means to walk to the park. Eventually this branch of the investigation ceased, producing no leads or valid suspects.

By mid-February, a series of sensational rumors arose fueled purely by the area's vicious homophobia. Whispers citing evidence that never existed and eyewitness accounts simply looking for their five minutes of fame circulated not from the humble residents of the *khrushchevki*, but from the panicked upper middle class. Suddenly past visitors to the park came out of the woodwork, claiming they saw the killer fleeing through the trees and describing him as a man in women's clothing and a wig. Yet another piece of gossip spread claiming some of the bodies had been raped and found with lipstick marks all over the face, neck, and body.

Demonstrating they are not immune to the rampant homophobia and transphobia of the people they protect, local police claimed an innocent victim to their witch hunt. Late at night on February 20th, someone whom the lead investigator later described as a middle aged transvestite was seen in Bitsa Park by police canvassing the area and whose mere presence was immediately deemed suspicious.

Accounts of what followed vary greatly, with many sources glossing over the resulting exchange entirely. Claims range from the suspect attempting to flee, mysteriously breaking free of handcuffs, to pulling a knife that was never found and threatening the policemen directly. One source described nearly 200 officers being called to the scene to detain this one person. The most agreed upon and substantiated elements of that night seem to be that the suspect had a hammer in their bag, and one thing led to another that resulted in police shooting the suspect in the leg and requiring hospitalization. It was later found that their "suspect" had corroborated, air-tight alibis for each of the murders and had done nothing wrong; the hammer had been for protection against the Maniac.

Apprehending the **Culprit**

Two months and nine bodies later, the police finally caught their break in the form of Marina Moskalyeva, the first victim since young Mikhail with direct ties to Pichushkin. Marina was a single mother to her 15 year old son and worked full time at the same grocery store as Sasha. Not only had they worked together, but when questioned after the fact, Marina's son described Pichushkin as her boyfriend and had met him before. Thanks to a subway ticket in the pocket of her jacket, police were able to easily find footage of Pichushkin meeting Marina at a metro station just outside Bitsa Park on the day of her murder. In case that had not been enough, Marina had left a note with her son saying she was going for a walk in the park, naming Sasha Pichushkin and even listing his phone number in case her son needed her.

Marina had known there was a killer at large in Bitsa Park and went anyway; likewise, Pichushkin knew Marina had left a note with his name and number, and still killed her. The man Marina knew—the shelf-stocker who lived with his mother, a man's man, a smoker and a drinker, her coworker—seemingly posed no threat. She had known him, trusted him enough to introduce him to her son. In the case of Pichushkin, investigators suggested that he craved the attention of getting caught, purposefully choosing a victim that would lead to his arrest. What seems more likely based on his confession, is that when given the opportunity to kill Sasha simply couldn't resist.

Within hours of being apprehended, Pichushkin confessed to not only Marina's murder and the twelve others the police are aware of, but claimed he had killed as many as 63 people. Plying him with sandwiches and cigarettes, detectives finally begin to understand the scope of the disappearances and consequent murders in and around the ignored *khrushchevki*. Following standard procedure for murder cases, Pichushkin is taken to the scene of the murders to reenact them on film, eventually to be used as evidence in his trial. Due to the extensiveness of his crimes, what is typically only a few hours of video continues on for nearly 40 hours filmed over the course of a month.

While Pichushkin's trial is much less of a spectacle than that of his idol, Chikatilo, it is still well publicized and attended by an aggravated crowd of his victims' families. Despite his fluctuating claims of 62 to 64 murders, the official charges brought to trial on September 13th are for 49 counts of murder and 3 attempted murders. Where police had ignored the voices of the lower class and their accounts of missing friends and families, the press steps in. With Sasha's quiet and undocumented past, journalists take statements from family members of victims, neighbors from Pichushkin's building, even random members of the community, stitching together a story for the Chessboard Killer, no matter how fabricated.

The most notable aspect of the trial was possibly the lack of controversy surrounding such a large and well-reported case. With very little deliberation, Pichushkin's psychological evaluation deemed him sane, stating that "his actions were purposeful and consistent... he was aware of what he was doing." After meeting for only three hours, the jury unanimously ruled Pichushkin guilty on all counts. Pichushkin's defense team filed an appeal within weeks but it was denied immediately. The first fifteen years of Pichushkin's life sentence were ordered to be spent in solitary confinement in a northern high security prison, where he remains today.

Despite the severity of his sentence, the prosecutors and the family of his victims are still divided in their opinions of his punishment. The chief prosecutor told the press immediately after the trial let out that he believed that "justice has been done... He received the punishment that he deserved." In contrast, Tamara Klimmova, whose husband fell victim to Pichushkin, demanded more.

"He should be handed over to the public for punishment rather than allowed to live in prison at our expense."

Now nearly nine years into his sentence, Pichushkin continues to serve out his punishment in solitary confinement. Sasha will be 44 years old when he integrates back into communal prison life, just another member of Russia's growing prison population of almost six hundred fifty thousand people, lost in the crowd of the criminal justice system.

SMELLY BOB

NATHAN HAYES

Robert Black (Smelly Bob)

Robert Black, also known as "Smelly Bob" was a Scottish pedophile and serial killer who preyed on young girls in the United Kingdom. Between 1981 and 1986, Black was convicted of the kidnap, sexual assault, and murder of four girls—plus the kidnapping and rape of another young girl and the attempted kidnapping of yet another—between the ages of five and 11 and was sentenced to life in prison with a minimum of 35 years. Black is also suspected of being responsible for the murders of 12 other girls between 1969 and 1987 in England, Ireland, and continental Europe. Black died of natural causes on 12 January 2016 while incarcerated at HMP Maghaberry, just weeks before he was to be charged with the murder of another of his victims.

Early Life

Robert Black was born on 21 April 1947 in Grangemouth, Stirlingshire, Scotland, the illegitimate son of Jessie Hunter Black who was 24 at the time and an unknown father whose name was never put on Black's birth certificate. Jessie earned a pittance as a factory worker and was in no position to care for a child, let alone an illegitimate one which carried with it a large social stigma. So, when he was six months old Black's mother had him fostered. He was subsequently raised by experienced, middle-aged couple Jack and Isabel Tulip who lived in Kinlochleven. Black initially adopted their surname and lived with them until 1958 when his foster mother died; his foster father having already passed away when Black was five. When Margaret died, Black was only 11 years of age.

In the meantime Black's mother married Francis Hall, had four more children who never even knew that they had a half-brother, and moved to Australia. She died in 1982 without ever having any contact with the son she gave away.

Locals remember how young Black was usually heavily-bruised as a child; however, Black himself does not remember how he sustained most of the injuries. He did recall how Margaret used to lock him in the house as punishment for poor behavior or would spank his bare bottom with a belt. During the night, Black feared that there was a monster under his bed and he suffered from a recurring nightmare that featured a "big hairy monster" in a cellar full of water. When he awakened, he found that he had typically wet the bed, for which he was invariably beaten.

In school he was referred to as "Smelly Robbie Tulip" and is remembered to this day as "aggressive and slightly wayward" as well as being a loner with a tendency to bully. Black preferred the company of younger children who he could easily dominate. Instead of joining a "gang" of classmates his age, he started his own and all of the members were several years younger than he. Compounding the problem was that Black demonstrated "sudden, mindless violence perpetrated against those physically less able than himself."

The local bobbie, Sandy Williams, remembers Black as a "wild wee laddie" who "didn't give a damn" or have respect for authority and that he had a "dangerous spirit" and "needed a smack round the ear to keep him in line." However, the entire time Black lived with the Tulips he was never in serious trouble; just childish fights, bullying younger children, swearing, and other normal trouble at school—nothing that merited more than a rebuke from Williams.

When Margaret died when Black was 11 years of age, it was one of the worst possible things imaginable because now he was, again, deprived of a mother. Black was subsequently placed with another foster family in Kinlochleven. He only lived with them a short time because not long after his placement he dragged a young girl into a public bathroom and sexually fondled her. His new foster mother reported the offense to social workers and insisted that Black be placed elsewhere. Black was then sent to the Redding Children's home, a mixed-gender children's home near Falkirk, close to where he was born.

From a young age Black exhibited significant antisocial tendencies, particularly a disturbing awareness of and fascination with sex and women's vaginas. At the age of five he and a girl compared their genitalia. At the age of seven at a school dance he preferred lying on the floor and staring up girls' dresses instead of actually dancing. At the age of eight he took off a neighbor's baby's diaper while he was babysitting to look at her vagina. Despite being heterosexual, Black stated that he would have preferred to have been born female; not that he had any feminine tendencies but he simply hated his penis and would have preferred having a vagina instead. In a prison interview after he was convicted for his heinous crimes, Black confessed to enjoy pushing things up his anus and following his arrest in 1990, police found photographs Black had taken of himself with various unusual objects inserted in his anus. He also confessed to a preoccupation with feces. If one attributed classical Freudian personality psychology, that Black had a tendency to withhold emotion, was oftentimes smelly and messy, and was preoccupied with his anus, then he would be the epitome of an anal personality type.

While in Falkirk, Black was reported as having exposed himself on a number of occasions and, one time, forcibly removing a girl's underwear. At the age of 12 Black made his "first inept attempt at rape." He and two other boys took a girl their age into a field, took off her knickers and lifted her skirt but none were able to "complete the act of penetration." Instead, they touched her vagina and Black admitted that he "forced her to some degree."

After the authorities were called—and had a conference with staff at the Falkirk home—Black was sent to the higher-discipline, all-male Red House in Musselburgh. During his stay there, a male staff member regularly sexually abused him and Black began to solidify his association of sex with dominance and submission.

While in school he developed interests in both swimming and football. Due to poor eyesight he was unable to become a footballer;

however, he was well suited as a lifeguard as he was an excellent swimmer. Further, the sight of young girls in swimsuits fueled his pedophilic fantasies. In fact, 20 years later, when Caroline Hogg was abducted and murdered, her house was en route between the two swimming pools where Black worked as a teenager.

In 1962, when Black was 15, he left the children's home and procured a job as a delivery boy for a butcher. He rented a room in a boys' home in Greenock, near Glasgow, and during this time he admitted to having molested as many as 40 girls while doing his delivery rounds. He claims that when he made a delivery if a young girl was home alone he would sit down and talk to her and then try to touch her.

His first conviction was for lewd and libidinous behavior with a young girl. In 1963, at the age of 17, he approached a seven-year-old girl in a local park and asked her if she would like to accompany him to see some kittens. The naïve girl followed him into a deserted air-raid shelter. He held her by the throat until she lapsed into unconsciousness and he both masturbated over her body and sexually fondled her. She was later found wandering the streets; bleeding, crying, and confused. Black admitted that he didn't know whether she was alive or dead when he left her. Instead of lewd and libidinous behavior, Black should have been charged with and tried for attempted murder. Prior to his 25 June court date, a psychiatric evaluation concluded that this incident was an isolated one and that Black did not need any further treatment.

Black then left Greenock and returned to Grangemouth to start over. After securing employment with a builders' company and renting a room, he finally met his first real girlfriend, Pamela Hodgson. After a physical relationship he fell in love and proposed; however, she broke off the engagement not long after. He was devastated.

In 1966, Black's inappropriate sexual desires resurfaced when he repeatedly molested his landlords' nine-year old granddaughter. While the girl reported it, no charges were filed but Black was asked to leave.

Black returned to his childhood home of Kinlochleven and took a room with a couple who had a seven-year old daughter. Again, he molested the young girl; however, this time the incident was reported and he pled guilty to three counts of indecent assault and was sentenced to a year at Polmont Borstal that was known for rehabilitating the worst of the juvenile criminals. Whereas Black had no problem reiterating all of the aspects of his life and crimes, he has never discussed his time at Borstal, thus leading many to speculate that he was abused during his sentence.

Six months after he was released, Black moved to London and his discovery in child pornography quelled his immediate desire to prey upon young girls. He had discovered that magazines such as *Teenage Sex* and *Lollitots* were clandestinely available, particularly in other countries where pornography laws were less strict such as the Netherlands and he traveled to Amsterdam on several occasions. In fact, when police searched his home after the murders they found over 100 magazines and 50 videotapes depicting child pornography; in addition to Black's own discrete photographs of girls between the ages of eight and 12 he had taken which he kept with his child pornography in a locked suitcase.

Between 1968 and 1970 he held various odd jobs including working as a swimming pool attendant. While here he would oftentimes go underneath the pool, remove the lights, and watch young girls swim. One girl reported that Black had touched her inappropriately and, while no charges were filed, he was fired.

While in London, Black spent considerable time playing darts in pubs—particularly the Three Crowns Pub in Stamford Hill—and became a decent player and a well-known face on the amateur circuit. Many recall Black as a loner who preferred to drink alone irritate others, particularly ladies. During this time Black became acquainted with a Scottish couple named Edward and Kathy Rayson who offered Black lodgings in their empty attic room, which he accepted. He was responsible, albeit reclusive, who—in spite of his poor hygiene—was a model tenant. Although Mrs. Rayson did suspect her lodger of being an avid viewer and reader of pornographic material, neither of the Rayson's thought the material was pedophilic. Black lived with them until his arrest in 1990.

In 1976, after purchasing a white Fiat Transit van, Black secured employment working as a driver for the Hoxton-based Poster Dispatch and Storage, Ltd. that specialized in delivering posters—primarily of music stars—and billboard advertisements. Black would work for PDS for ten years until he was fired due to his constant minor car accidents that cost the company considerable money. Shortly after his dismissal, the company was purchased by two employees who rehired Black because even though he continued to get into accidents, he was a hard worker and was happy to cover for his coworkers by taking the longer runs others didn't care for as they interfered with family commitments. Disturbingly, Black kept a variety of masturbatory tools and girls' clothing which he would don and reenact fantasies in his head; particularly replaying the incident with the seven-year-old girl he had left for dead. When Black committed his first murder it seemed to him like the perfectly natural progression from the fantasy he replayed so frequently.

During his employment, Black became thoroughly familiar with many of London's streets, particularly its minor ones, which would enable him to easily abduct young girls and dump their bodies far from their home without witnesses.

Also during this period, Black changed his appearance multiple time; from shaving his head, growing and/or shaving a beard, and wearing a multitude of different glasses.

The Crimes

Jennifer Cardy, 9

Jennifer Cardy was abducted, sexually assaulted, and murdered on 12 August 1981; a mere two weeks after her ninth birthday. The young girl was last seen by her mother at 1:40 p.m. when she left her house in the County Antrim village of Ballinderry to ride her bicycle to her friend Louise Major's house. When Cardy didn't return home her family telephoned Major's parents where they were informed that their daughter had never even shown up at their house. Cardy's parents called the police and a search for the missing girl was immediately implemented.

Cardy's bicycle—covered with leaves and branches—was discovered an hour later less than one mile from her home. The kickstand of the bicycle was downwards which suggested that, perhaps, Cardy had stopped to talk to someone—likely her abductor—however, there were no witnesses.

Six days after Cardy's disappearance, two hunters found her body in a dam located close to a dual carriageway in Hillsborough, just 15 miles from her home. Her body displayed evident signs of sexual assault and the autopsy concluded that she had died of drowning that was most likely accompanied by ligature strangulation.

Susan Maxwell, 11

On 20 July 1982, 11-year-old Susan Maxwell from Cornhill on Tweed on the English/Scottish border left her home on her bicycle to play tennis in Coldstream. The two-mile route ensured that Maxwell would know most everyone she passed on the way and it was an area where people looked out for each other, especially the children. A number of local witnesses remembered seeing her until she crossed the bridge spanning the River Tweed.

Maxwell's mother Elizabeth reported her daughter missing after she had driven to the tennis courts to pick her up. One of her daughter's friends said that the two girls parted company outside of the Coldstream police station to walk home their separate ways.

The next day a full-scale search began, involving police and search dogs from both sides of the border. At the height of this search, over 300 officers were assigned full time to locate the young girl with activities including canvasing houses in the area and thorough searching every property within the two towns; over 80 square miles of terrain.

While there were no witnesses to the actual abduction, several people described a white van in the area.

An autopsy concluded that Maxwell had died shortly after her abduction; however, the exact date and time of death remains unknown. Maxwell remained in Black's van, whether alive or dead, for 24 hours as his delivery schedule took him into Edinburgh, Dundee, and Glasgow, where he is known to have made his final scheduled delivery at around midnight. The following day, Black returned from Glasgow to London, and discarded Maxwell's body in a copse near the A518 road near Uttoxeter, Staffordshire; 264 miles from where she was abducted.

On 12 August, Maxwell's body was found by Arthur Meadows, a lorry driver, in a ditch near the A518 road at Loxley, near Uttoxeter, in the Midlands; 250 miles from where Maxwell had been abducted. Her body was fully clothed except for her underwear and shoes and her body had been covered with undergrowth. Due to the advanced state of decomposition, she was identified by dental records. The exact date, time, and cause of death could not be determined. What was known, however, was that Maxwell had been bound, her mouth had been gagged with sticking plaster, and her underwear had been removed and neatly folded beneath her head; thus indicating that she had likely been sexually assaulted before her murder; however, the state of the body precluded knowing for sure what, exactly, happened.

Caroline Hogg, 5

Nearly a year later, five-year-Caroline Hogg became Black's youngest known victim. She disappeared while playing in a park near her Beach Lane home in Portobello—a suburb of Edinburgh—in the early evening of 8 July 1983 after begging her mother Annette for "just five more minutes" of playtime. When Hogg had not come home by

7:15 p.m. her parents and brother looked for her. A young boy around Hogg's age said that he had seen her in the company of a man on the nearby promenade, which her mother and brother frantically searched to no avail. Her mother then called the police and reported her young daughter missing.

An intensive search was undertaken which, at that time, was the largest ever in Scottish history. 2,000 local volunteers and 50 members of the infantry regiment Royal Scots Fusiliers searched all over Portobello and neighboring areas; all the way to Edinburgh. The search also attracted considerable local and national media coverage. In fact, by 10 July, the young girl's disappearance was headline news across the entire United Kingdom. Police interviewed the nine known pedophiles who were in Portobello on the night Hogg disappeared but they were all cleared.

Several eyewitnesses had seen an dirty looking, "bald man who wore glasses" watching Hogg as she played before following her to a nearby fairground named Fun City. 14-year-old Jennifer Booth saw Hogg sitting on a bench with this strange man. Booth heard Hogg reply, "Yes please," to some question posed by the man and assumed that they were father and daughter as they walked toward the fairground while holding hands. At Fun City, the man paid 15 pence for Caroline to ride the children's carousel as he watched her. Afterward, she left the fairground in his company. One child witness stated that she had seemed frightened

Not unlike his other victims, Hogg remained in Black's van for at least 24 hours and her exact date, time, and cause of death remains unknown. Black's schedule showed a poster delivery to Glasgow several hours after Hogg's disappearance and he refueled his vehicle in Carlisle in the wee hours of the following morning.

Hogg's naked body was found on 18 July in a ditch off the A444 road between Northampton to Coventry and close to the M1 motorway in Twycross, Leicestershire; 301 miles from where she had been abducted and a mere 24 miles from where Maxwell's body was discovered the previous year.

Due to advanced decomposition, Hogg was identified by her hair band and locket. The exact cause of death was undetermined; however, the entomologist who examined the body asserted that the body could not have been dumped prior to 12 July, thus suggesting that Black may have disposed of her body while making a delivery to Bedworth on the same date. That she was found completely naked also strongly suggested that her murder was sexual.

The following March, a televised reconstruction of Hogg's abduction was broadcast nationally with the hopes of producing further eyewitnesses. Additionally, all parking tickets issued in Edinburgh were examined, tourists as far as Australia were asked to send in rolls of camera and cine film they had taken in Portobello, police sat for weeks by the A444 taking down registration numbers of all vehicles that passed, and investigators searched the homes of all men identified as having been on the promenade that night for "immoral purposes." After the broadcast, Hogg's parents appealed to the public for any anonymous tips to help them find who killed their daughter. Her father said, "You think it can never happen to you, but it has proven time and time again that it can, and it could again if this man isn't caught in the near future."

Sarah Harper, 10

Three years later, ten-year-old Sarah Harper disappeared from Morley, Leeds, at approximately 7:50 p.m. on 26 March 1986, after she left her home on an errand to purchase a loaf of bread from a local market, the K&M, a mere 100 yards from her home. The shop's owner, Mrs. Champaneri confirmed that the girl did, in fact, purchase a loaf of bread and two packages of crisps at approximately 7:55 p.m. and left at 8:05 p.m. She also stated that a balding man entered her store moments later and left when Harper left.

Harper was last seen by two girls walking into an alley leading towards her Brunswick Place home; a shortcut that locals used. When she had not returned by 8:20 p.m., her mother, Jackie, and sister, Claire, briefly searched the surrounding streets before reporting the young girl missing to West Yorkshire Police at approximately 9:00 p.m. Police—as in the other cases—immediately launched an extensive search for the child with over 100 police officers being assigned full-time to look for the young girl. This search involved house-to-house canvases across Morley; the search of over 3,000 properties; distribution of over 10,000 flyers; and the taking of 1,400 witness statements. Additionally, another 200 local volunteers helped search surrounding areas including the search of a reservoir in nearby Tingley by underwater units.

West Yorkshire Police confirmed that a white Transit van had been seen in the area where Harper had been abducted while two suspicious men had been seen in the vicinity near where Harper walked to the store. One of them was a stocky, balding man. Believing that Harper had likely been abducted the police sent a telex to all forces nationwide requesting that they search the areas where other child murder victims had been found.

At a 3 April press conference, Harper's mother Jackie told journalists that she believed her daughter was dead but that the worst thing was not knowing. Appealing to the abductor, Jackie said, "I just want her back, even if she's dead. If someone would just pick up the phone and tell us where the body is." Afterward, Jackie fainted.

On 19 April, while walking his dog, a man named David Moult found Sarah's naked body, gagged and bound, floating in the River Trent near Nottingham, nearly seventy miles from where she was kidnapped.

An autopsy revealed that while the cause of death was drowning, she sustained injuries to her head and neck which likely rendered her unconscious before she was thrown into the water. In addition to being beaten, the evidence demonstrated that Harper had been the victim of a violent and sustained sexual assault—including being sodomized—prior to being tossed into the river. The pathologist described these pre-mortem injuries as "simply terrible." The young victim's father, Terry, Jackie's ex-husband, had to identify his daughter's body and stated that "it was worse than I ever dreamed of."

Investigation and Arrest

By the spring of 1983, whereas many detectives assigned to the inquiry into Maxwell's murder were assigned elsewhere, several detectives did, in fact, remain on the case. When Hogg's body was found in July 1983, Detective Chief Superintendent of Staffordshire Police Dennis Boden held an emergency meeting with senior Staffordshire and Leicestershire detectives to explore the possibility that the same person was responsible for both murders.

Cardy's murder would not be formally linked to the other cases until 2009.

Due to the distance between where the victims were abducted and subsequently found, police suspected that the same person was responsible and that he worked in an occupation that required extensive travel across the United Kingdom, such as a lorry or van driver, or some type of sales representative. Additionally, that both victims were bound and likely subjected to sexual assault—and were clad in white ankle socks when they disappeared—it was presumed that this triggered some sort of fetish response by the perpetrator. It was also decided that due to the circumstantial and geographical nature of the crimes that the perpetrator was likely an opportunist.

Further, since both Maxwell and Hogg were abducted on a Friday, the perpetrator most likely had some sort of delivery or production schedule. After discovery of the bodies, police contacted all transport firms with deliveries in Scotland and the Midlands and all drivers were questioned as to their whereabouts on the dates of the abductions; however, this tactic failed to uncover any potential leads.

Complete cooperation existed between police from the four separate police departments involved in the manhunt. Initially, a satellite incident room that was based in Coldstream coordinated the collective efforts for leads in the Maxwell case while additional incident rooms in Leith and Portobello coordinate the search for evidence in Hogg's case. However, within hours of the discovery of Hogg's body, there was overwhelming consensus that both cases were linked and that they should join efforts with one investigating officer to coordinate all inquiries. Assistant Chief Constable of Northumbia Police Hector Clark was appointed to lead the investigation. Clark established incident rooms in Northumberland and Leith police stations to coordinate all efforts to search for the girls' murderer.

Initially, all information related to both cases was logged with a card-filing system that initially grew to over 500,000 index cards just for the Maxwell case alone. Being familiar with the criticism levied against police during the Yorkshire Ripper case for their being overwhelmed due to the sheer volume of information filed with this type of system, Clark introduced computerized technology into the investigation. Collective use of a computerized database that everyone involved in the investigation could access would improve results. Thus, by December 1986, all of the information related to the three murders (thus far) would be entered into the HOLMES information technology system and additional information would continue to be entered so that police forces nationwide would be able to cross-check all data entered into the system. Initially, detectives looked at individuals who had been convicted of serious sexual crimes against children within the ten years prior to Maxwell's murder in 1982 be further investigated. The list of potential suspects was narrowed to 40,000; however, Black's name never arose as his only conviction was in 1967.

Eventually, this database that was based at the Child Murder Bureau in the West Yorkshire city of Bradford would expand to hold information on over 187,000 individuals; 220,000 vehicles; and 57,000 witness interviews. Much of the information in the database had been obtained through three confidential hotlines established in 1984 by the inquiry team which eventually enabled police to solve numerous other, unrelated crimes, including child abuse offenses.

Several days after Harper's abduction and murder, a witness contacted West Yorkshire Police to inform authorities that on 26 March, at approximately 9:15 p.m., he had seen a white van parked close to the River Soar. A stocky, balding man was standing by the passenger door. Because the River Soar is a tributary to the River Trent and that the vehicle's and man's descriptions were similar to those given by other witnesses, investigators took this account seriously. Furthermore, Black is known to have refueled his van in the Newport Pagnell, Buckinghamshire, the following afternoon; which may suggest that he had taken Harper to the village of Ratcliffe on Soar and had discarded her body in the river either in the evening of the day she was abducted or in the early hours the following morning. Because Harper's abductor likely traveled on the M1 motorway before disposing of her body, investigators from both West Yorkshire and Nottinghamshire Police Departments questioned motorists and staff at all service stations along the M1 motorway between Woolley and Trowell as to whether they might have seen anything unusual on the 26th or 27th of March. Staff at one service station did, in fact, remember a white Transit van that had "seemed out of place" on the evening of 26 March; however, they could not provide a clear description of the driver.

Clark initially did not believe that Harper's murder was connected to Maxwell's and Hogg's due to several dissimilarities; however, in retrospect there were glaring and perhaps more telling similarities. All of the victims were young girls skillfully abducted from public places for sexual purposes and they were driven south and murdered. Further, the three bodies were found within 26 miles of each other in a triangular area known as the Midlands Triangle. Even though Harper's sexual assault appeared to be more vicious than the other two, experts assert that serial killers frequently increase their violence as the murderer gains more confidence and requires more brutality to achieve and maintain arousal. Eight months after Harper was found, Her Majesty's Inspector of Constabulary determined that all three murders were, in fact, linked and that one database be established. Entering all information into a single database took three years and was completed in July 1990.

In 1986, investigators formally requested assistance from the FBI to create a profile of their perpetrator which was completed in January 1988. This profile described the killer as a 30- to 40-year-old white male, likely a loner, who would likely be unkempt in appearance and had received less than 12 years of formal education. He probably lived alone, rented his home, and was in a middle-class neighborhood. Additionally, the profile surmised that the murderer's motives were purely sexual and that he likely had a fixation or obsession with child pornography. Profilers also hypothesized that the killer retained souvenirs from his victims and likely engaged in necrophilia with his victims' bodies shortly after their deaths.

Black was arrested on 14 July 1990, near Stow, Scotland, after snatching six-year-old Mandy Wilson off of the street and bundling her into his van. An alert neighbor, 53-year-old retired postmaster David Herkes, took down the van's registration number and called the police. After a chase, Black was apprehended. The victim was actually the daughter of one of the police officers on the scene and he discovered his daughter in the back of the van, bound and gagged, and stuffed into a sleeping bag. Prior to tying her up, Black had sexually assaulted her. Black was charged with plagium (kidnapping).

When Black's residence was searched, investigators discovered a large collection of child pornography.

Trial and Sentencing

In August 1990, Black was tried and convicted of kidnapping Wilson and given a life sentence. The sentence was based, largely, upon psychiatrists' testimony that Black would continue to pose a great threat to young girls.

Black was still the prime suspect in the murders of Susan Maxwell, Caroline Hogg, and Sarah Harper. Clark decided to interview Black as he was already serving a life sentence for the Wilson kidnapping and Clark mentioned that when he first saw him his gut feeling was that Black was his man. However, instinct and a gut feeling are not good enough for procuring a guilty conviction in a court of law. Black spoke candidly about his prior convictions, about his short relationship with his fiancée, about the sexual abuse he had endured as a child, about his fantasy life, and about his masturbatory practices. When asked specific questions about the three murders he fell silent.

A check of Black's gas receipts and delivery schedules placed him in the vicinity of each girl's abduction and he was charged with all three murders, as well as the attempted kidnapping of a 15-year-old girl who had escaped from the man who tried to drag her into his van in 1988. In this case, on 28 April 1988, 15-year-old Teresa Thornhill had been walking home from the park where she had met friends when Thornhill noticed a blue van stopped ahead. When the driver asked her for help and she denied, he had grabbed her from behind and was taking her to his van. She recalled that he was sweaty and stinky and was able to grab his testicles while screaming. Her friend Andrew, hearing her screams, came to help his friend and chase the assailant away.

Black's murder trial began on 13 April 1994 in front of Judge William MacPherson. Black pled not guilty to the ten charges levied against him which included murder, kidnapping, and preventing the lawful burial of a body. Despite his denial of any guilt, the prosecution was able to place him at each scene and to demonstrate similarities between the three murders and the prior kidnapping for which he had already been convicted and sentenced. His trial lasted five weeks.

On 19 May, the jury found Black guilty of all charges and he was sentenced to life imprisonment with a minimum of 35 years for each charge, to be served concurrently; thus rendering him 82 years old before being eligible for parole—if he were still alive at that time.

On 15 December, Black had been served a formal summons charging him with the murder and sexual assault of Jennifer Cardy and his second murder trial began at Armagh Crown Court on 22 September 2011 before Judge Ronald Weatherup. As he did regarding his other three victims, Black pled not guilty.

Evidence such as gas receipts and delivery schedules demonstrated that Black was in the area at the time Cardy disappeared. This second trial lasted six weeks and on 27 October 2011 he was found guilty of abducting, murdering, and sexually assaulting Cardy. He was given another life sentence.

Aftermath

Black suffered a fatal heart attack while incarcerated at HMP Maghaberry on 12 January 2016, just weeks before he was to be charged with the murder of 13-year-old Genette Tate who had disappeared while delivering newspapers on 19 August 1978 in Aylesbeare, Devon, England.

Senior detectives believe that Black was responsible for eight deaths, in addition to the Tate case; however, 12 other child murders committed across the UK, Ireland, and continental Europe between 1969 and 1987 have also been linked to Black. These include: April Fabb, 13, 8 April 1969, UK; Christine Markham, 9, 21 May 1973, UK; Suzanne Lawrence, 14, 22 July 1979, UK; Patricia Morris, 14, 16 June 1980, UK; Pamela Hastie, 16, 4 November 1981, UK; Mary Boyle, 6, 18 March 1977, Ireland; Silke Garben, 10, 20 June 1985, Germany; Cheryl Morriën, 7, 5 August 1986, Netherlands; Virginie Delmas, 10, 5 May 1987, France; Hemma Devy-Greedharry, 10, 30 May 1987, France; Perrine Vigneron, 7, 3 June 1987, France; and Sabine Dumont, 9, 27 June 1987, France. In all of these cases, Black is known to have been in the area or a white van with a driver who resembled Black was seen.

Prior to his death, Black never admitted culpability in any of the murders for which he was convicted and suspected.

His body was cremated on 29 January and his ashes were discarded at sea.

The Footpath Murderer

Natalie Avalon

Colin Pitchfork (Footpath Murderer, Black Pad Killer)

Colin Pitchfork, also known as the Footpath Murderer and the Black Pad Killer was born 23 March 1961 in Bristol, England. Because Pitchfork's two murders occurred in Leicestershire, the two murders have sometimes been referred to as the Enderby Murders or the Narborough Murders.

The early 20-something Pitchfork—a local baker by trade who was married and had two small sons—was tried, convicted, and sentenced to life for the rape and murder of two 15-year-old girls, Lynda Mann and Dawn Ashworth. He was also convicted for other, earlier, indecent assaults and attempting to pervert the course of justice by enlisting a friend to provide a DNA sample in his place. In fact, Colin Pitchfork has the dubious distinction of being the first person in the world to be convicted with DNA evidence—a new technology at the time. This case is also notable for being the first time where a suspect was cleared based upon DNA testing.

Early Life

Colin Pitchfork was born in Bristol, England, on 23 March 1961, the second of three children, to a housewife mother and miner father. His parents were married and raised all three of their children; however, Pitchfork was oftentimes neglected for affection by his parents who favored his older sister and younger brother over him.

Pitchfork was raised in Newbold Verdon and attended school in Market Bosworth and Desford. While in school Pitchfork was teased because he had matured considerably quicker than his classmates.

In 1979, at the age of 18 he was arrested and convicted of indecent assault after pulling a 16-year-old girl off of a country lane. Instead of indecent assault, his actions could have been more accurately classified as attempted rape. Pitchfork was subsequently referred for therapy at Carlton Hayes Hospital, Narborough, on the Black Pad footpath. The hospital was subsequently closed in 1996; however, the path remains.

He had never served time in jail or prison until he was arrested for murder.

In October 1985, Pitchfork dragged another 16-year-old girl into a garage and "indecently assaulted" her while threatening to kill her with a screwdriver. After he was arrested for the two murders, he pled guilty to and was convicted of the assault; however, that he forced his victim to perform oral sex on him is now correctly defined as rape.

On yet another occasion he picked up a blonde hitchhiker named Liz who ended up grabbing the steering wheel in an effort to escape, thus forcing him to release her before he got the chance to rape her.

In 1981 when he was 20 years old, Pitchfork married Carole, a social worker, and the couple moved to Littlethorpe. Also that year Pitchfork obtained psychiatric counseling at the Woodlands for his sexual proclivities.

The Pitchforks eventually had two sons. The first was born in 1983 and the second in 1986; interestingly the same years Pitchfork committed his two murders.

Carole confessed that while she was pregnant, her husband had become "unsettled" and had resorted to complaining about everything. He was a "the grass is always greener" type who never valued what he had. He would oftentimes say that he wanted a different job, or a bigger house, or something other than what he had. In fact, this extended to his sex life. Despite being married and his wife expecting a baby—twice—Pitchfork often cheated on her. During Carole's first pregnancy, it was a woman named Leslie. Pitchfork had the audacity to bring her over to meet his family, introducing her as a "friend from work." With her second pregnancy it was a woman dubbed "Brown Eyes." She was in the midst of a divorce and already had a child. This was in July 1986 right before Pitchfork's second murder. He had been feeling depressed and went to see a doctor for sleeping pills. The reason for his depression was that "Brown Eyes" was pregnant with his child. He did, however, always want a daughter as his two sons with Carole were obviously not enough so, while depressed, he was also looking forward to having a daughter.

One of Pitchfork's early jobs was as a volunteer at Dr. Barnardo's Children's Home before obtaining long-term work in Hampshire's Bakery in 1976 as an apprentice. He continued to work at the bakery until he was arrested for the murders. His forte was as a cake decorator, particularly sculpting decorations and he had aspirations to start his own cake decorating business someday. His supervisor touted Pitchfork as a "good worker and time-keeper" but "was moody...and he couldn't leave women employees alone." He earned a reputation for talking to and directing considerable attention toward female coworkers, which was oftentimes unwelcomed.

The Crimes

Lynda Mann, 15

15-year-old Lynda Mann was a quiet schoolgirl who enjoyed school and showed a talent for art. On a frigid night, 21 November 1983, Mann went to visit her friend Karen. After leaving Karen's house at approximately 7:30 p.m. she was never seen again. After Mann failed to return home, her justifiably worried parents called the police.

Pitchfork was driving his infant son home when he saw Mann walking along Forest Road near the Black Pad footpath. When she entered the footpath, he parked his car, caught up with her, and exposed himself. Scared, she attempted to run from him but Pitchfork caught up with her and raped her on some land adjacent to the footpath before strangling her to death with her own scarf.

He murdered Mann to prevent her identifying him. He admitted to police that before he raped her, she had said, "What about your wife?" which indicated that she had seen his wedding ring and knew he was married. He also knew that he was wearing an earring and had realized he was losing his hair; both of which could help Mann identify him. He also told investigators that, at the time, he was planning on moving to Littlethorpe, near Narborough—Mann's hometown—and that there was a great likelihood that she would see him in the area. Thus, he decided that he ought to murder her and tie up that nasty loose end that could potentially get him arrested.

The next morning, Mann was found raped and strangled on the Black Pad footpath that was situated between a cemetery and Carlton Hayes Psychiatric. Her clothes were strewn about and she was strangled with her own scarf.

The forensic evidence—most notably lack of any bruising or other pre-mortem injuries—suggest that Pitchfork first strangled Mann and then raped her as evidenced by the lack of pre-mortem injuries, despite the medical examiner's findings that Mann had been brutally raped.

When 22-year-old Pitchfork attacked Mann, his infant son was asleep in the back seat of his car. He raped and strangled her before driving home and putting his son to bed.

Semen was collected from the body and it was determined that the perpetrator was a secretor which means that his blood type is identifiable in other bodily fluids. It was determined that the murderer had type A blood with a +1 phosphoglucomutase (PGM) enzyme. This profile was applicable to approximately ten percent of adult males in England at the time which led to the police DNA dragnet that will be discussed later.

Dawn Ashworth, 15

On 31 July 1986, 15-year-old Dawn Amanda Ashworth took a shortcut home along a footpath known as Ten Pound Lane on her way home from her job at a newsstand in Enderby. In addition to her parents, she had a younger brother named Andrew.

Ashworth was a student at Lutterworth Grammar School—the same school that Lynda Mann attended. She enjoyed drawing and painting and was very good at them both. Ashworth also liked clothes and music like most teenage girls. Attractive and likeable, Ashworth had many friends, in addition to a reputation as a sensible and mature girl for a 15-year-old.

On that fateful evening, Pitchfork was riding his motorbike and saw Ashworth enter the footpath. He then parked his bike and followed her, caught up with her, and then exposed himself to her. Ashworth tried to run from him but Pitchfork was able to catch her. He raped her in a field adjacent to the footpath.

Not unlike Lynda Mann, Pitchfork murdered Ashworth to prevent her from identifying him. Also like Mann, he strangled Ashworth with her own scarf and then hid her body under some loose foliage.

Two days later on 2 August her body was found a mere mile from where Lynda Mann's body was found three years ago and like Mann, she had been raped and strangled. Ashworth's body was "buried" under heavy brush and hay. However, Ashworth's body contained considerable pre-mortem injuries, thus suggesting that she put up a considerable struggle against her assailant and was raped before she was murdered.

Semen samples taken from Ashworth's body matched the semen taken from Mann's body.

After Pitchfork murdered Ashworth, he returned home and baked a cake.

Ashworth was buried in the cemetery behind St. John the Baptist Church in Enderby in a plot adjacent to where Lynda Mann was buried, thanks to church administrators who offered the Ashworths the plot.

Despite Ashworth's case being reenacted and featured on *Crimewatch UK* in December 1986, police failed to identify and apprehend the assailant because of the lack of evidence to link Pitchfork—the real murderer—to the victim or the crime.

Investigation

Former 14-year Los Angeles Police Department officer turned best-selling author Joseph Wambaugh wrote a book about the Pitchfork case entitled *The Blooding* (1995) that details the crimes, the advent of DNA testing, and the difficulties faced by the police in investigating the crimes. Many of the quotations in this discussion are from Wambaugh's book.

Police, under the leadership of Chief Superintendent David Baker, examined all of the similarities of the two cases: both occurred along relatively obstructed-from-view footpaths; the victims were both teenage girls walking alone; they were both raped and strangled; they were from the same area, even attending the same school, as previously mentioned; and their bodies were found in similar conditions and close to one another. They concluded that the same person murdered both girls before forensics proved this fact.

DNA Profiling

The initial prime suspect in the case was 17-year-old Richard Buckland; a local youth with learning disabilities who worked in the kitchen at the local psychiatric hospital not far from the two footpaths where the girls were found. He was considered to be the prime suspect because he had revealed knowledge of Ashworth's body and the crime scene; information that only the killer would know as it wasn't anything in the papers that the general public would be aware of. He also could not account for his whereabouts during the time when Ashworth was killed. After a lengthy and grueling 15-hour interrogation, Buckland finally confessed to Ashworth's murder but repeatedly denied having anything to do with Mann's murder three years earlier. In all actuality, he would have only been 14 at the time anyway. Nevertheless, despite all of Buckland's protestations, police believed that he killed both girls.

The DNA samples were taken to geneticist Dr. Alec Jeffreys at the University of Leicester. Along with Peter Gill and Dave Werrett of the Forensic Science Service (FSS), the three men developed the earliest form of DNA testing and detailed the technique in a 1985 paper. In it, Gill stated that he was responsible for developing the DNA extraction techniques and demonstrating that it was, in fact, possible to obtain DNA profiles from old stains. Of particular interest and usefulness in the Pitchfork case was the capability of developing "the preferential extraction method that was able to differentiate sperm cells from vaginal cells to facilitate the use of DNA evidence in cases of sexual assault."

Dr. Jeffreys said that he accidentally discovered DNA fingerprinting—what he called it—while researching hereditary diseases and concluded that—like fingerprints—an individual's DNA was completely unique; except for identical twins who shared the same DNA as they shared the same fingerprints. He used the restriction fragment length polymorphism (RFLP) technique which seeks to identify and exploit the variations in homologous (or similar) DNA sequences. In this type of analysis, a DNA sample is divided into pieces which have restriction enzymes added to them and the resulting fragments are then separated by gel electrophoresis according to their lengths. The procedure, at the time, was relatively inexpensive and enjoyed widespread application, such as in the Pitchfork case where officers obtained genetic samples from every male in the area where the murders occurred whose blood matched the killer's blood type that was identified because he was a secretor and his blood type was available through the semen he left inside of his victims. Historically, RFLP analysis was a critical tool in genome mapping, in localizing genes to identify genetic disorders and to determine risk for disease, and in paternity testing. The Pitchfork case was the first time DNA testing was used in a criminal case.

Using the preferential extraction method, Dr. Jeffreys compared semen samples collected from both Mann's and Ashworth's bodies and further analysis demonstrated that both girls were, indeed, killed by the same man. The testing also proved that Buckland was not the murderer and he was subsequently cleared and released.

Of course, the police were mildly irritated because they believed that the murderer was in custody and they had little faith in this new science. After contacting the FSS and having another analysis done, the results corroborated Dr. Jeffreys' findings. Thus, Buckland became the first person in history to have his innocence proven through DNA fingerprinting. Dr. Jeffreys added that he had "no doubt whatsoever" that Buckland would have been found guilty without the definitiveness of DNA testing.

Buckland was released after serving four months in jail.

The question remains as to why had Buckland confessed. Some speculate that he likely found the body which is how he knew some information that was not made available in the news. This, coupled with the relentless pressure of an exceedingly long and grueling interrogation made him yield under pressure.

The Blooding

Now that Buckland had been cleared, the search for the real murderer began. The FSS and Leicestershire Constabulary initiated a DNA dragnet in which 5,000 local men were asked to volunteer blood and saliva samples with the hopes of finding the real murderer. This process is referred to as "blooding" and was from where Wambaugh got his book's title. This investigation manhunt targeted all local men between the ages of 16 and 34. After six months, the police were no closer to identifying and apprehending the offender than they had been at the outset.

Pitchfork wholeheartedly believed in the science of DNA testing and used his cunning and conniving mind to formulate a way out of the testing. He enlisted the assistance of a friend, Ian Kelly, who was not required to test as he did not live in the targeted area, and got him to donate his DNA in Pitchfork's place. The two men got passport photos of Kelly and Pitchfork expertly swapped the photo in his own passport. He had done such a good job that the police did not suspect a thing; something for which they would be criticized later.

After Kelly gave the sample for Pitchfork, the latter had to "make it look good"; that he, in fact, was tested. Pitchfork, therefore, scratched a mark on his inner forearm with a compass needle and then applied an adhesive plaster. When he got home that afternoon, Carole commented that she thought it would only be a pinprick but Pitchfork, ever the exaggerator, made a huge brouhaha about, first, removing the plaster which he did as though he were removing sutures, and second, how much his arm hurt.

When the letter came that told Pitchfork that he was not, in fact, the murderer, Carole was extremely relieved. But her relief would prove to be short-lasting.

Arrest

Pitchfork may have not been apprehended for some time save for a stroke of luck. On 1 August 1987, while drinking at a Leicester pub, Pitchfork's friend and coworker, Ian Kelly, confessed to others that Pitchfork had given him £200 for giving a DNA sample while pretending to be Pitchfork. Allegedly, Pitchfork had told Kelly that he had already given his sample under another friend's name because that friend had a prior conviction for burglary when he was a youth and wanted to avoid any police harassment. Since Kelly was not a local man, he was not part of the investigation and, therefore, not required to volunteer a biological sample. Had it not been for a woman sitting nearby who had overheard the conversation and reported it to the police, Pitchfork would not have been identified and arrested, and more women would have likely been raped and murdered.

Pitchfork was arrested at his home on Haybarn Close in Littlethorpe on 19 September 1987. The officers waited for his blue Fiat to enter the cul-de-sac and for the family to enter the house safely. Then Derek Pearce and Gwynne Chambers went around the house to cover the back door. The "two Micks"—Mick Thomas and Mick Mason—went to the front door and Phil Beeken and Brian Fentum backed up the two Micks. At 5:45 p.m. Thomas knocked on the door. Carole answered, initially believing them to be insurance agents. When they entered the house the two Micks identified themselves as police officers who needed to speak to her husband privately.

Mason asked Pitchfork, "Why Dawn Ashworth?" Pitchfork replied, "Opportunity. She was there and I was there." When Pitchfork spoke to his wife, she asked him if he did, in fact, murder the two girls. He admitted that yes, he was. She flew at her husband, beyond angry, and had to be stopped by Thomas before inflicting any serious harm upon her husband. She did manage to punch Pearce in the mouth and kick him in the groin.

In the police car Pitchfork told the officers, "I *must* let a few people know what's happened to me before they read it in the papers," and then, he said, he would tell them everything. He added, "[I]t's really a story of my life, not just the story of a month of two."

A DNA sample taken was found to match the murderer. He was the 4,583rd man tested in the England DNA "blooding" dragnet.

Pitchfork admitted that he had flashed females in excess of 1,000 times during his life and that this behavior was a compulsion started when he was in his early teens. He stated that flashing led to sexual assault which led to strangling in order to protect his identity.

With respect to the Ashforth murder, investigators had asked myriad questions and the entire time Pitchfork was being questioned he acted like he was being put out and that investigators were insulting his intelligence. He had said that he initially thought he ought to rob his victim because he saw ten pounds in her purse but then thought better of it because he wasn't sure how he would explain ten quid to Carole.

Police confronted him about the brutality of his rape of Ashworth as she was "torn up pretty badly." They asked if he knew that she was a virgin and Pitchfork said that she told him halfway through the rape. They also asked him about injuries to her bottom and asked him if he knew what he had done. Pitchfork had said that he wasn't in complete control over what he was doing but that he "can *relive* it second by second." Again, obviously annoyed like any reasonably-adept sociopath when confronted with other people's consciences which he views as a weakness, Pitchfork admitted that he knew that he was "talking about it coldheartedly."

He also added that Ashworth "died a damn sight quicker than Lynda Mann" because, with Mann, he didn't go straight for her carotid artery to cut off the blood flow to her brain. Pitchfork added that doing so was a recognized Japanese way of killing and that he'd been trained in judo and would any of the interrogators like for him to demonstrate the technique on one of them. They were not impressed with his stories.

Pitchfork also told investigators that he lost his watch at the scene and inquired as to whether anyone found it.

Throughout the interrogation investigators noticed that Pitchfork would leave out pertinent details about his activities that would make him appear unmanly or something like that. For example, when asked about his flashing over 1,000 girls in his youth he vehemently denied that he masturbated in front of them and any mention of premature ejaculation was immediately shut down. Pitchfork also blamed Mann and Ashworth for walking through open gates on their own, just inviting trouble, while he tried to let them pass. He would also never admit that he sodomized Ashworth.

Trial and Sentence

The day after his arrest, Pitchfork was taken to his first remanding at Castle Court, an old English court that looked like one would imagine it to; complete with stone walls and oak pillars, arched windows, and some blackened ceiling beams that dated back to 1105 A.D. Brian Escott-Cox was the prosecuting barrister, David Farrer was Pitchfork's defense counsel, and Mr. Justice Philip Otton oversaw the proceedings.

Pitchfork was charged with and confessed to two murders, as well as two additional separate indecent assaults from 1979 and 1985, and he also admitted attempting to pervert the course of justice by enlisting Kelly to provide his own DNA sample on Pitchfork's behalf. Pitchfork pled not guilty to the kidnapping of Liz, the hitchhiker, who he had "spared" for some reason that even Pitchfork could not accurately iterate.

Farrer said during the hearing that Pitchfork would be "forever haunted by the images and knowledge of what he has done"; however, the court psychiatrist stated that the hauntings of a psychosexual sociopath does not constitute horror but "inspiration." The psychiatrist classified Pitchfork as an opportunistic, non-compulsive, sexual sociopath who only decides to offend when he sees a potential victim. This differs from those sexual serial killers who stalk their victims or who have a specific "type" for whom they look.

Justice Otton, upon Pitchfork's sentencing, stated that the rapes were particularly sadistic and had it not been for the advent of DNA testing, there was a great likelihood that Pitchfork could still be free and many other women would be in danger. Otton sentenced Pitchfork to two life sentences for the murders, ten years for the two "indecent assaults" in 1979 and 1985, and three years for "perverting the course of justice" by evading the DNA testing and getting Ian Kelly to submit his DNA in his place." Per the Home Secretary, Michael Howard, Pitchfork's minimum term, or tariff, was set at 30 years, which meant that Pitchfork would have to serve at least 30 years before becoming eligible for parole. After an appeal, Pitchfork's sentence was reduced by two years.

Ian Kelly was given an 18-month suspended sentence for his part in conspiring with Pitchfork to hide his DNA.

After the sentencing, the media wanted to interview Dawn Ashworth's family but they denied the request. Instead, an older interview with the family during the investigation was aired in February 1988. In this old footage, Ashworth's mother Barbara stated—when asked about potentially forgiving her daughter's murderer— that she has to forgive or she would feel "very bitter and twisted" and that's not a way to live. Her father Robin said, "I don't feel any hate or wish for any revenge for the murder of Dawn, because it's not going to do any good." However, once Pitchfork was sentenced and the DNA evidence proved conclusively that Pitchfork was, in fact, the murderer, Robin said that he wanted the death penalty reintroduced. Further, in a public poll, 96% of the public was in agreement for bringing back the hangman in cases such as this.

Lynda Mann's mother and stepfather, Kath and Eddie Eastwood, as well as her sister Rebecca Eastwood, have been vocal about how Pitchfork should never be paroled. In fact, Rebecca created an online petition specifically to halt any potential parole hearing should one actually arise seeing as how Pitchfork is scheduled for a parole hearing sometime in 2016. As of January 2016, Rebecca has collected 17,000 signatures, much to her own surprise and delight.

Baker was also interviewed following Pitchfork's sentencing as the police were under considerable scrutiny for their failure to identify and apprehend Pitchfork earlier. Baker was asked why Pitchfork was never questioned given his flashing background. He was also criticized for his people allowing an altered passport to get by them—this passport being the one that Pitchfork "adjusted" with Ian Kelly's photograph. Other questions included why Pitchfork wasn't fingerprinted and photographed in all of his previous brushes with the law. Baker had said that one reason was that, at the time, flashing was considered only a nuisance and not a "real" crime. Baker also added that the victims of Pitchfork's earlier assaults would likely not have been able to pick his mugshot out of a photo parade because the assaults occurred late at night and Pitchfork altered his appearance by growing or shaving facial hair.

Appeal

On 14 May 2009, Pitchfork's appeal was heard at the Royal Courts of Justice in London. He was granted a two-year reduction to his original 30-year sentence. Consequently, Pitchfork was eligible to apply for parole in September 2015 due to the time served spent upon remand prior to his conviction and this was postponed until early 2016. However, the Lord Chief Justice stated that Pitchfork could not be released "unless and until the safety of the public is assured."

Since he has been incarcerated, the 52-year-old Pitchfork has educated himself to degree level and had achieved proficiency in the transcription of printed music into Braille with the hope, one day, of being able to help the blind. His defense team presented this evidence as indication of the development of Pitchfork's character while incarcerated.

Aftermath

Artwork and Sales Proceeds Controversy

In April 2009, a sculpture that Pitchfork had created in prison was exhibited at the Royal Festival Hall on London's South Bank. The artwork—called "Bringing Music to Life"—depicted an orchestra and choir made "in meticulous miniature detail by folding, cutting and tearing the score of Beethoven's Ninth Symphony." The sculpture was purchased by the Royal Festival Hall for £600 and was subsequently exhibited as part of a venture by the Koestler Trust that was originally founded by novelist Arthur Koestler and runs an awards contest for inmates. Initially presented anonymously, when the sculptor's identity was finally revealed in April 2009, the revelation was met with both astonishment and anger from crime victims' groups. Compounding the problem was that Pitchfork profited financially from the sale of his sculpture; earning £300 of the sale proceeds himself. Per the Trust's policy, the artist receives half of the sale proceeds, the charity retains 40% themselves, and 10% goes to victim support.

However, outrage in the *Daily Mail* due to Pitchfork's past and why he had been incarcerated led to the sculpture's removal; particularly since he had fashioned it while incarcerated at Frankland Prison, Brasside, Durham. Pitchfork's caption for the sculpture was, "Without this opportunity to show our art, many of us would have no incentive, we would stay locked in ourselves as much as the walls that hold us."

Lynda Mann's mother Kath said that "paying her daughter's 'evil, wicked and cruel' killer of his work showed a 'lack of conscience.'" She added that he is in prison as punishment for his horrendous crime and for violating Rawls' social contract theory and that should never be forgotten. Additionally, Kelvin Donaghey—a family friend of Dawn Ashworth—created a memorial website to both Ashworth and Mann. He stated that both girls were very good at art and they never got the chance to see their own work exhibited; however, the man who brutally murdered them gets to display his own plus earn compensation from it and that was wrong. In response, Tim Robertson, chief executive of the Koestler Trust stated that the person's offense is irrelevant as the quality of the art is more important. He added that the charity makes no distinction between artists' crimes but only releases their names when given written permission by both the inmate artist and the Prison Service. However, the charity failed to obtain that permission. Eventually, Royal Festival Hall officials removed the artwork from display and apologized for any ill-will harbored and any offense caused and while it respected the Trust's policy, future policy would, indeed, be reviewed.

Those who see no problem with the arrangement state that if an inmate is attempting to rehabilitate himself and improve his life while incarcerated then society "should be pleased by that rather than condemning him or trying to stop him from benefiting from the proceeds." In fact, Pitchfork is not the only criminal to profit from prison-produced art. East End gangster Ronnie Kray painted a series of eight landscapes on prison issue cards while incarcerated during the 1970s which subsequently sold for £16,550 at auction. Additionally, Jimmy Boyle—"the most violent man in Scotland"—became a prison sculptor and later wrote his own autobiography which was later made into a film entitled *A Sense of Freedom* (1981). Further, Charles

Bronson, also known as Charles Arthur "Charlie" Salvador and born as Michael Gordon "Mickey" Peterson—"Britain's most dangerous inmate" and the topic of the 2008 film *Bronson*—has received at least 11 Koestler awards for his poetry and art.

Pitchfork's cunning, however, rests upon the fact that his art unveiling coincided with an upcoming High Court appeal to demonstrate that he could be a productive and upstanding member of society. Ongoing criticism ensues, particularly with the potentially offensive title of his work—"Bringing Music to Life"—as well as the message beside the sculpture Pitchfork penned.

In 2014, a two-part television miniseries entitled *Code of a Killer* was commissioned and broadcast in two 90-minutes episodes on 6 and 13 April 2015. It was based on Pitchfork's crimes and the creation of DNA profiling. The program starred John Simm and Dr. Jeffreys, David Threlfall as Baker, and Nathan Wright as Pitchfork.

Dr. Alec Jeffreys was knighted by the Queen in 1994.

THE BRILLIANT SERIAL KILLER : THE TRUE STORY OF ISRAEL KEYES

MARK TOLBERT

Israel Keyes was an American serial killer who was active from approximately 2001 to his capture in 2012. He was known for his extreme attention to detail, his patience and discipline in selecting targets that lived far away from him. He was also meticulous in disposing of his victim's bodies as authorities have not uncovered any other evidence that Keyes did not provide.

Keyes killed several victims across the United States and was finally caught in 2012 after he uncharacteristically deviated from his modus operandi and hatched a plan to collect a ransom from his last victim's family.

Keyes was known to go to extreme lengths to hide his involvement in these murders, including driving across the country in rental cars, while using nothing but cash and removing the batteries from his cell phones in order to evade detection. This is uncharacteristic for a serial killer, since the vast majority of his contemporaries are known to have killed within their general geographic area.

While in federal custody in Anchorage, Alaska, Keyes would cooperate with investigators and admit to a host of crimes, including kidnapping, rape, and murder. Furthermore, Keyes admitted to committing a variety of burglaries and bank robberies to fund his killing sprees.

Early Life

Israel Keyes was born in Richmond, Utah in 1978. He was the second child to John Jeffrey Keyes and Heidi Hokansson. John, a maintenance man, and Heidi, a stay-at-home mom, raised their son in a Mormon environment and home-schooled both Israel and his eight siblings.

Soon after his birth, Israel's parents moved the family to Aladdin Road, a small area north of Colville, Washington. While his family officially followed the Mormon faith, they were known to attend a local Christian Identity church, an organization rumored follow a white supremacist version of Christianity. Some, however, dispute this label and liken the religion to having parallels with the Amish church.

The family also quickly became friends with the neighbors, the Kehoe family. Chevie Kehoe, the eldest of eight sons, would later become an infamous white supremacist and convicted murderer, after killing William Frederick Mueller, along with his wife and daughter, during a robbery to secure guns, ammunition, and money.

During his time in Aladdin Road, Israel became a very introverted child with little interaction with the other children in town. He built his own cabin at the age of sixteen and preferred the wilderness over people. He is known to have burglarized several houses during his time in Aladdin, however, and is believed to have killed family pets for entertainment.

"When I was fourteen there was some friends staying with us," Keyes recalled. "And there was this cat of ours that was always getting into the trash. I had a lot of guns and I would always carry a gun and I shot it in the stomach. And it ran around and around the tree...and then it like crashed into the tree. I actually kind of laughed a little I think but..and then I looked over at everybody else and the kid who was with me, he was throwing up. Like he was, really, I don't know (chuckles) traumatized I guess you would say."

"Like most serial killers," forensic psychiatrist Paula Orange said. "Keyes built himself up to killing people by killing small animals first."

Following his family's relocation to Smyrna, Maine to become involved in the maple syrup business in the late 1990s, Keyes was kicked out of his family home for rejecting his parents' faith. His parents told his siblings to stay away from him.

"Keyes didn't think too much of his family," Orange said. "He was raised in a cult-like atmosphere and rejected the family religion, becoming very outspoken out his lack of belief in God. He had a Satanic pentagram branded on his back as well as an upside-down cross on his chest."

The rejection made Keyes want to tour the country and burn down as many churches as he could. Instead, he turned to murder and rape.

His first violent crime was committed sometime between 1996 and 1998, when Keyes abducted a teenage girl and raped her. Despite his later penchant for murder, he allowed this victim to go free. The identity of the teenage girl remains unknown.

Military Career

In 1998, Israel Keyes decided to enlist in the United States Army while living in New Jersey. Keyes served as a specialist in the 1st Battalion, 5th Infantry. He was subsequently stationed at Ft. Lewis, near Tacoma, Washington, and at Ft. Hood, near Killeen, Texas. He would later receive training in the Sinai region of Egypt.

While serving in the U.S. Army, Keyes was awarded the Army Achievement Medal for "meritorious service while assigned as a gunner and assistant gunner from the 2nd of December 1998 to the 8th of July, 2001 in the Alpha Company 60mm mortar section." Although Keyes received a DUI in Washington state in May 2001, he left the U.S. Army with an honorable discharge later that year.

Keyes would settle in Alaska and get a job working in construction. Incredibly, he would draw rave reviews from his employer who had no idea of the double life his new carpenter with the long hair led.

"Keyes was described as someone who was very professional," Orange said. "He had a tremendous focus and would work on projects for hours on end with intensity and focus. He would not stop for lunch. He would just work straight on through."

Keyes was described in a favorable manner by just about everyone else who met him. Words like "friendly", "low-key", "reliable" were among the adjectives used to describe him.

"The secret life was power to Israel Keyes," Orange said. "He got off on the fact that everyone he encountered had no idea who or what he really was. To them, he was a friendly carpenter who was on the quiet side. Mellow. But inside he was a raging killer. That is what gave him power."

Crimes

Bill & Lorraine Currier

After receiving his honorable discharge from the United States Army, and sometime between April and May 2011, Israel Keyes constructed a homemade silencer for his Ruger .22 pistol. Once he decided to kill, Keyes booked a flight from Washington state to Indiana. After arriving in Indiana, Keyes rented a car and drove the remaining 1,000 miles to the East Coast of the United States, using cash-only for the duration of the trip to avoid leaving behind any evidence.

Keyes arrived in New York to test his homemade silencer, then traveled to Vermont to pick up a murder "toolkit" that he had buried two years before. Keyes soon found an abandoned farmhouse in Essex, Vermont, which he identified as the location he would take his next victim to before killing them. He initially targeted random drivers passing through the rural area, intending to shoot out a tire on their car and kidnap them after they crashed, but decided to focus on a married couple after dismissing his original plan as unpractical and dangerous.

He soon identified Bill and Lorraine Currier, living at 8 Colbert Street, as his next victims on July 8, 2011.

Bill and Lorraine were 49 and 55 years old respectively. They had just celebrated their 25th wedding anniversary. Bill worked at the local university as a lab assistant while Lorraine worked at a nearby medical center.

"They were good people," Orange said. "They had a lot of pride in the upkeep of their Vermont home, manicuring the lawn and planting flowers. They were good employees and well-liked by co-workers. They were the epitome of upstanding, normal good people."

Keyes had picked the Currier's because they had no dog, no kids and a garage that would let him into the house. He stalked them for days, knowing their comings and going.

As one investigator would note, "Keyes was a serial killer with a system."

In the middle of the night, Keyes disabled the Currier's phone line and entered their house in what has been described as a "blitz attack." He ambushed the couple while they were sleeping and quickly subdued them, tying the couple up and stealing Lorraine's .38 snub-nose revolver in the process.

Once the couple was secured, he proceeded to transport them to the abandoned farmhouse in Essex. During the course of the night, both Lorraine and Bill attempted to escape the house. Lorraine was successfully captured and re-restrained. However, Keyes shot Bill with his silenced .22 caliber Ruger pistol in a fit of rage during his escape attempt. After killing Bill, Keyes sexually assaulted Lorraine and strangled her to death in the basement.

Following the killings, Keyes buried Bill and Lorraine's bodies in the basement of the Essex farmhouse, intending to return to the house at a later date to set fire to the building and thereby destroy any evidence in the blaze. Once the bodies were buried, Keyes set out to commit a robbery spree using the Currier's car.

"Keyes was spotted driving the Currier's car," Orange said. "The eyewitness quickly relayed this information to the police and they were able to come up with a sketch of Keyes. They were reported missing by this time and the authorities knew that foul play was involved. Things became particularly worrisome as the man in Currier's car was driving alone and the couple was nowhere to be found."

The Currier's car soon suffered "serious mechanical issues" and Keyes decided not to go through with his crime spree.

Keyes quickly abandoned the Currier's non working car in an apartment parking lot at 203 Pearl Street and proceeded to the White

National Monument Forest to burn the couple's belongings and to bury his toolkit and handgun.

Unbeknownst to Keyes, the farmhouse containing the Currier's bodies was bulldozed from October 25-27, 2011. The bodies, along with the rest of the farmhouse, were unknowingly disposed of at the local landfill.

The resting place lived up to Keyes' motto, 'Out of sight, out of mind.'

Samantha Koenig

On February 1, 2012, Keyes began to search for another random victim. He identified 18-year old barista Samantha Koenig, living and working in Anchorage, Alaska, as his next victim.

Samantha worked at a walk-up kiosk on a relatively busy highway. It was snowing that night, however, and folks were driving by too fast to pay attention to the man who walked up to the counter in a ski mask. This would not be unusual in Anchorage as the weather was freezing. Samantha greeted Israel with a smile and he handed her his travel mug, asking for some coffee. She would turn back around he had a gun pointed at her.

"Turn out the lights," he commanded.

Samantha complied.

"Turn around," he said.

Samantha began to cry, complying with his command. He forced her to empty the register then tied up her wrists with cable wire. After finding out that Koenig had a boyfriend who was set to show up soon, Keyes laid in wait for the boyfriend, Duane Tortolani. However, he quickly abandoned his plan to capture a second victim and dragged Koenig to his truck before transporting her to his property.

The next day, February 2nd, Keyes broke into Koenig's house. While there, he also burglarized her boyfriend's truck, taking the couple's joint debit card with him. However, both Koenig's father and Duane Tortolani witnessed this burglary and notified the authorities.

Keyes quickly tested the debit card to make sure that it worked and, upon confirming that it worked, he returned to his home and quickly killed Koenig, leaving her body in a storage shed located on his property. He immediately traveled to New Orleans, where he set out on a week-long cruise. However, once he disembarked from the cruise Keyes became increasingly concerned over the media coverage and intense police investigation of Keonig's disappearance and set out on a crime spree.

On February 16, Keyes burglarized and burned down a home in Aledo, Texas. Shortly thereafter, Keyes robbed the National Bank of Texas, attempting to kidnap yet another woman he saw walking a dog. Luckily, this potential victim was able to escape.

Other Victims

Israel Keyes is suspected of killing or attempting to kill several other victims. Keyes' first admitted violent crime took place sometime between 1996 and 1998, when he abducted and raped a teenage girl in Washington state. Unlike his later crimes, Keyes did not kill this victim. He released her soon after the sexual assault.

"My entire goal was to stay under the radar," Keyes said. "For a lot of this stuff, there wasn't anything. All I can say is that unless I talk about it, you're never going to find any evidence."

His first suspected murder is of an unknown couple in Washington State in 2001. Keyes also claimed to have killed another unidentified victim in Leah Bay, Washington in July 2001.

He planned out his killings like most people plan out their vacations. He would travel far away from his location.

From 2005 to 2006, Keyes is suspected of killing two separate victims. He confessed to these murders while being held at the Anchorage Correctional Complex, saying that these murders were committed on two separate occasions. Furthermore, he claimed to have dumped one of the bodies in Crescent Lake, located in Oregon.

"There is a history of this stuff that goes back a long time," Keyes said. "It's not something I've ever talked to anyone about."

Keyes just didn't rape his female victims. He would rape his male victims as well. It was something he was ashamed of as well as his necrophilia.

Following a multi-year break from killing, Keyes admitted to killing Debra J. Feldman in Hackensack, New Jersey on April 8, 2009. He also claimed to have killed another victim the following day somewhere in New York state.

Keyes would bury his murder weapons across numerous fields across the entire United States. Because of his military training, he knew how to maintain the weapons and return to them after they had been out of use for years. He buried these weapons in canisters filled with cable ties, ropes and drain cleaner.

During these trips, Keyes would admit to frequenting prostitutes.

Lastly, following the murder of Samantha Koenig and during his travels throughout the Southwestern United States, Keyes claims to have killed an unknown victim in Texas. The identity and final location of this victim remain unknown.

In addition to the actual murders that he committed, Keyes admitted to attempting to kill several other individuals over the years. For example, Keyes admitted to attempting to shoot both a couple and male police officer in Anchorage, Alaska sometime between April and May 2011. He also admitted to attempting to kidnap and kill a woman he spotted walking her dog in Texas, just days before his capture by a combination of Texas and federal law enforcement.

Other Crimes

Keyes was known to commit burglaries and bank robberies in order to fund his killing sprees. In addition, he admitted to killing small animals from the time he was a young child. He is said to have killed an unknown number of family dogs and cats throughout his travels.

April 10, 2009

Keyes robbed the Community Bank in Tupper Lake, NY in order to fund his killing spree. After holding up the bank teller with a .40 caliber Smith & Wesson (and with a .22 caliber 10/22 Ruger pistol in reserve), Keyes made off with over $10,000 in cash. Although he was filmed on camera during the robbery, his use of sunglasses, uncharacteristic clothing, and a fake mustache prevented him from being identified.

Following the successful robbery, Keyes buried a box with his robbery supplies in the Woodside Natural Area in Essex, Utah. He returned home four days later with the $10,000 in his possession.

<u>February 16, 2012</u>

While Keyes was traversing across the Southwestern United States following the successful ransom for Samantha Koenig, he committed two additional crimes. First, Keyes committed arson by setting fire to and burning down a 3,500 square foot house in Aledo, Texas. Secondly, Keyes again committed a bank robbery by holding up a teller at the National Bank of Texas in Azle, Texas, making off with an undisclosed amount of cash.

In all, Keyes is suspected of committing some 20 to 30 home invasions and burglaries during his lifetime. Furthermore, he killed an unknown amount of animals from his childhood to capture and is believed to have committed several unidentified bank robberies during his adult years in order to fund his killing trips across the country.

Capture

After murdering Samantha Koenig and leaving Alaska, Keyes concocted a plan to demand a $30,000 ransom for Koenig's return (at the time, police were unaware that Koenig had been killed). Keyes texted his demands and instructions to Duane Tortolani, Koenig's boyfriend.

At the same time, Keyes dug up the body of Samantha Koenig, dismembered it, and disposed of the body in Matanuska Lake.

The case became a high-profile one and community members chipped in to meet the ransom demand.

Thirty-thousand dollars, courtesy of a concerned and frightened community, would be deposited into Samantha's account.

After receiving the ransom money, Keyes began withdrawing cash from the associated account using her stolen debit card. There would be withdrawals in Alaska. Then Arizona. Then New Mexico.

The authorities would always be fifteen minutes behind the suspect when he made these withdrawals.

Israel would wear a "Scream" mask while the withdrawals but his 2012 Ford Focus that he was drawing was identified. The FBI noted all of their counterparts to be on the lookout for Keyes in this vehicle. It is important to note that Keyes actually exchanged his rented 2012 Ford Focus for another car to avoid detection; however, the rental company provided him with another 2012 Ford Focus for his exchange. This would eventually help to lead to his capture.

Police were then able to track account withdrawals as he traveled throughout the Southwestern United States, having made withdrawals from Koenig's account using her debit card in New Mexico, Arizona, and Texas. Interestingly, authorities had a video of Koenig's abduction but refused to release the footage to the public, a controversial move that many outsiders saw as hampering his capture.

Having left his sister's wedding just days before (where he became embroiled in a contentious argument about his pronounced atheism), Keyes was spotted speeding along Highway 59 by a Texas Highway Patrolman on March 13, 2012.

"The patrolman that made the traffic stop had no idea that Keyes was a wanted serial killer," Orange said "Keyes did not have his gun handy at the time. If he had, there's no doubt in my mind that he would have started shooting."

Keyes was placed under arrest by the patrolman and the Texas Rangers as well as the FBI was brought in. Authorities found the following items in Keyes' possession at the time of his capture: Koenig's ATM card and cell phone (with the battery removed), a ski-mask, handgun, and bundles of rubber-banded cash that was traced to the recent National Bank of Texas robbery.

The authorities still had hope that Samantha was still alive.

But Keyes would tell them nothing. He stared straight ahead without emotion as detectives hammered him with questions. Authorities would get very little out of him. He was thirty-four years old and lived a quiet life with his girlfriend and ten year old daughter in Anchorage. Everything about Keyes' past seemed normal. But he had a creepy withdrawn nature about his personality. When the FBI searched his property, they found out why.

He had searched numerous time on his computer for Samantha Koenig. The FBI would then confront Keyes with the surveillance footage they had of his truck pulling up in front of the kiosk.

"We know it was your truck," the FBI agent said.

Keyes would remain silent for about forty seconds before he finally spoke.

"Well, I might as well tell you everything. She's dead."

Keyes revealed that he had used a needle and thread to open up Samantha's eyes as she posed with the newspaper in the ransom photo.

Keyes would recount how he brought Samantha back to his home and tied her up. He had a glass of wine before he began verbally taunting Samantha by telling her what he was going to do to her. He then raped the victim and choked her to death.

Only twenty feet away, his live-in girlfriend and ten year old daughter were sleeping. They would wake up the following morning and he would join them at the breakfast table. Like turning a switch on-and-off, he spoke of taking his family on a cruise.

"It was apparent that neither his girlfriend or his daughter knew of his crimes," Orange said. "He would tell investigators that 'no one really knew him.'"

Shortly after Keyes' capture in Lufkin, he was then extradited to Alaska to stand trial for Koenig's murder. His trial was set for March 2013 and he was slated to be represented by federal defender Rich Curtner. Keyes was thirty-four years old at the time of his arrest.

Investigation

Israel Keyes was officially extradited to Alaska on March 26, 2012. Shortly after arriving at the Anchorage Correctional Complex, Keyes confessed to the murder of Samantha Koenig, providing information which allowed investigators to locate her dismembered body on April 1st of the same year.

Keyes was initially willing to cooperate with authorities and offered to confess and plead guilty to all charges leveled against him if two terms were met: his trial would last no longer than one year and he would be given the death penalty. He also conditioned his cooperation on the basis that his name and certain details not be released to the media and public.

"I'm not in this for the glory," Keyes told interrogators. "I'm not trying to be on TV. I want my kid to have a chance to grow up. She's in a safe place now, she's not going to see any of this. I want her to have a chance to grow up and not have this hanging over her head."

In June 2012, Keyes attempted to violently escape from a courthouse in Anchorage, in what authorities suspected was a spur-of-the-moment suicide attempt. Keyes was successfully subdued with a taser and taken back into custody alive. Following his attempted escape, Keyes was placed on a suicide watch, which entailed a prohibition on razor blades and sharp objects, regular inspections of his cell, and a 24/7 guard.

The next month, in July 2012, a local news station, WCAX, reported Keyes' connection to the kidnapping and murder of the Curriers. This lead to Keyes ending all cooperation with the authorities for the next two months.

Modus Operandi

While cooperating with authorities at the Anchorage Correctional Complex, Keyes described his approach to killing thusly: "I would let them come to me... You might not get exactly what you're looking for, there's not much to pick from, so to speak. But there's also no witnesses, there's nobody else around."

Location

Israel Keyes was very methodical in his approach to killing. Unlike most serial killers, Keyes did not kill victims who lived near him. Most serial killers conduct most of their kidnapping and abductions within the vicinity of their home, which leads to an easier investigation and higher chance of being captured. Keyes, on the other hand, was known to take cross-country trips in order to kill.

For example, Keyes killed the Curriers in Vermont while he was living in Washington state. Once he decided to kill, Keyes booked a flight from Washington to Indiana. He then rented a car, removed the battery from his cell phone, and paid for all of his expenses with cash as he drove 1,000 miles to the East Coast. He tested his homemade silencer in New York, retrieved a murder toolkit that he had hidden in Vermont two years earlier, and then identified the Curriers as his next victims. This type of careful planning, attention to detail, and restraint is very uncommon in serial killers.

Victim Profile

Unlike most serial killers, Keyes did not have a specific victim profile. For instance, Ted Bundy, another serial killer who shared many qualities with Keyes, was known to target young, white women between the ages of 15 and 25. However, Keyes had no such victim profile. He alternatively killed or attempted to kill married couples, young woman, men, and several other unknown victims. This allowed him to operate without substantial police scrutiny for some time.

Method of Killing

With the exception of his killing of Bill Currier, Keyes strangled every one of his victims. Furthermore, Bill Currier was shot to death while attempting to escape from the house that Keyes was keeping him and his wife at. Had Bill not been killed in the heat of passion while attempting to escape, it is likely that Keyes eventually would have strangled him to death as well.

Death

After accidentally being provided with razors while on suicide watch, Keyes committed suicide on December 2nd, 2012. He sliced his wrists vertically and hung himself while being held at the Anchorage Correctional Complex. He was pronounced dead immediately.

Prior to committing suicide, Keyes composed a four-page, handwritten letter that was found underneath his body. The letter was covered in blood and was largely illegible, but FBI forensic investigators were able to reconstruct much of his letter.

While the letter did not provide additional details about his crimes and victims, it did offer a glimpse into his psyche and reasons for committing murders. Keyes wrote "Family and friends will shed a few tears, pretend it's off to heaven you go. But the reality is you were just bones and meat, and with your brain died also your soul." Later in his letter he elaborated, "You may have been free, you loved living your lie, fate had its own scheme crushed like a bug, you still die." He repeatedly referred to his victims as a "pretty captive butterfly."

Dr. Stephen Montgomery, a forensic psychiatrist at Vanderbilt University Medical Center analyzed the letter and reached the following conclusion: "It has no remorse, no regard for human life or the victims and that fits with that type of psychopathic personality."

Authorities are still investigating various unsolved disappearances throughout the various states that Keyes visited. It is now believed that he may have targeted homeless shelters where he could kill people who would not be missed.

RAILROAD KILLER

They called him the 'Railroad Killer.'

Angel Resendiz earned the nickname because of his penchant for committing his crimes near railroads, using the rail cars as his own personal get-away system.

Committing murder after murder, he was able to elude both American and Mexican authorities for over a decade.

EARLY LIFE

A birth certificate found by the FBI listed his date of birth as August 1st, 1960. He was born To Virginia de Maturino in the town of Izucar de Matomoros in the state of Puebla, Mexico. His mother has stated adamantly that the correct spelling of his surname is Recendis not Resendiz although the killer would have over fifty different aliases throughout his lifetime.

Angel had spent his childhood years with relatives and not with his immediate family. According to his mother, he was sexually abused by an uncle and other pedophiles in the town of Puebla. He would spend his youth roaming the streets, robbing, stealing and sniffing glue. Relatives would later testify that Resendiz was routinely beaten as a child, one time being "jumped" by several other youths who beat him so bad that he bled through his ears. Resendiz would leave home for months at a time then suddenly return mumbling about a coming religious apocalypse.

Legal trouble came early for Resendiz as he was caught trying to sneak into the Texas border at the age of sixteen. This would become the first of numerous run-ins with border patrol agents until he finally made it into the United States, making his way to St. Louis and finding work with a manufacturing company under an assumed name. He even registered to vote with his false identification.

In September of 1979, at the age of nineteen, Resendiz was arrested for assault and car theft in Miami. He was tried and sentenced to twenty-years in prison but was released after only six years and sent back to Mexico.

But he wouldn't stay there for long.

Through numerous attempts of trial and error, Resendiz had learned not only to game the system but to enter and exit the United States with minimal detection.

He learn to use the rail-cars...

AN "INVISIBLE" MAN

Resendiz became so skilled at crossing the border without detection that he began charging for his services. He began to make a living as a human smuggler, transporting Mexicans across the border for a fee.

Resendiz soon developed a reputation for his smuggling skills, often being seen as a 'go to' person in his Ciudad Juarez neighborhood called 'Patria.'

He would make weekly crossings over the border, being arrested only intermittently. He would then be deported back into his native land only to ping-pong back and forth.

Finally, Resendiz would serve prison terms for his crimes. He would be arrested in Texas for false identity and citizenship, getting a year and half worth of jail.

Upon release in 1987, he journeyed to New Orleans and was arrested for carrying a concealed weapon. He received another year and half worth of prison time until parole.

He then went back to his old haunts in St. Louis where he tried to defraud Social Security and receive illegal payments. He got caught and served a three year sentence.

Resendiz then decided small-time burglaries were his deal. He once again illegally crossed the border, journeyed to New Mexico and was caught burglarizing a home. He was imprisoned for eighteen months and upon release he broke into a Santa Fe rail yard, being captured yet again.

"They should have called Resendiz the boomerang man," forensic psychologist Frank Lizzo said. "He knew how to play the game and seemingly had no fear of the system. The system never punished him severely enough for him to stop his crimes, let alone stop crossing the border."

After his last recorded deportation, the killings began.

THE KILLING FIELDS

"He probably started killing somewhere in his late 20s," Douglas said. "He may have killed people like himself initially – males, transients...(he) became angry at the population at large. What America represents here is this wealthy country where he keeps getting kicked out...(he) just can't make ends meet. Coupled with these feelings, these inadequacies, fueled by the fact that he's known to take alcohol, take drugs, lowers his inhibitions now to go out and kill."

Angel's list of victims began in 1986. Continuing to bounce in and out of the United States, he shot a homeless woman and left her for dead in an abandoned farm house. He had met the acquaintance of the woman at a homeless shelter and they became friends. They would later take a trip on a motorcycle together when he felt that the woman disrespected him.

Resendiz would then take out his gun and blow her head off.

The woman allegedly had a boyfriend whom Resendiz shot and killed as well. He said that he dumped his body in a creek between San Antonio and Uvalde. This killing has never been verified aside from what Resendiz revealed to the police during his interrogation sessions.

Five years later, Resendiz would kill Michael White because he was a "homosexual." Resendiz would bludgeon White to death with a brick and leave him in front of an abandoned home.

These were seemingly warm-ups for the more brutal crimes to come which would also include rape.

"Sex seemed almost secondary," FBI profiler John Douglas said when apprised of Resendiz's crimes. "(He is) just a bungling crook ...very disorganized."

Douglas would later concede, however, that it was this disorganization that worked in his favor. Like a true drifter, Resendiz' whereabouts became as elusive as a rational thought in his head.

"When he hitches a ride on the freight train, he doesn't necessarily know where the train is going," Douglas said. "But when he gets off, having background as a burglar, he's able to scope out the area, do a little surveillance, make sure he breaks into the right house where there won't be anyone to give him a run for his money. He can enter a home complete with cutting glass and reaching in and undoing the locks."

"He'll look through the windows and see who's occupying it. The guy's only 5 foot-7, very small. In fact...the early weapons were primarily blunt-force trauma weapons, weapons of opportunity found at the scenes. He has to case them out, make sure he can put himself in a win-win situation."

Resendiz would also leave his weapon of choice up to chance. Whatever the home would have, a statue a mantle piece, a butcher knife, that would become the instrument of murder.

FLORIDA KILLINGS

On March 23rd, 1997, Jesse Howell would be found bludgeoned to death beside the railroad tracks in Ocala, Florida. He was nineteen years old.

"When we got there," Sheriff Patty Lumpkin said. "We see what appears to be a young male, in his late teens or early twenties. Blood around the head area. You could tell by looking at him that he was dead. The first thing I do is make sure that we've got our forensics people on the way, on the medical examiners on the way, and all the investigators that we have called out or either there or en route."

"When those types of things happen it might have been someone who had fallen off a train," Lt. Jeff Owens said. "Or someone who could have been struck by a train."

The authorities quickly ruled out an accident, however, as they examined the body.

"It didn't appear to be an accident," Lumpkin said. "Because if he had been hit by the train the trauma would have been much more extreme. I've seen some deaths from trains and the initial impact from the train would have done more harm to the body."

The forensic team did determine that Howell's body looked as if he were the victim of blunt force trauma.

"We did see a baseball type of cap," forensic scientist Michael Dunn said. "It appeared to have blood on the inside surface of he bill. In addition, there was a pair of wire rimmed eye glasses and one of the eye pieces was missing, one of the lenses was out. This didn't look good either. As we moved closer, we saw that the victim had been dragged to that spot using just the blue jean material around the cuff (of his pants)."

Near the body, they found a brass and rubber coupling. This device was used to link one train car to another. It could also be used as a clubbing weapon.

"It had what appeared to be blood on it (the coupling)," Dunn recalled.

Howell still had jewelry on his person. He wore a gold cross necklace, a watch and a small amount of cash in his pocket. The police ruled out robbery as a motive.

The police did not identify Howell's body right off the bat. They did find a money wire receipt where some money had been wired from Illinois to Florida. The name on the receipt was of a woman named "Wendy."

Police tracked the money transfer to its point of origin which was all the way in Woodstock, Illinois.

Coincidentally, the authorities there were investigating the disappearance of Wendy Von Huben.

Wendy was missing alongside her boyfriend, the nineteen year old Jesse Howell.

"They advised me that they were investigating a John Doe," Woodstock Detective Kurt Rosenquest recalled. "Unidentified male."

Rosenquest then followed up with the investigating team in Florida, sending them the fingerprints and pictures of Jesse Howell.

The Ocala police would then positively identify Howell.

Jesse had met Wendy only months earlier. They had secretly planned to marry and went on a road trip with another couple.

The other couple, however, grew tired of Jesse and Wendy's constant bickering. They demanded to be let out of the car and left. Jesse and Wendy continued into Ocala, Florida where they ran out of money.

Wendy would call her parents in Illinois who would then transfer her $200 via Western Union. The couple would collect the $200 but would not return home.

"We checked Greyhounds," Rosenquest said. "Nobody matching their description ordered buses or train tickets back to the Woodstock area."

Tears were shed as Rosenquest informed Howell's parents that their teen son had been murdered. The investigative team then turned their attention to the disappearance of Wendy.

They held out hope because there were issues between her and Jesse, thinking that perhaps she simply ran off to be by herself.

Police scoured the surrounding areas and used helicopters in all directions around the railroad tracks.

They would find nothing. There was no DNA left behind on Jesse Howell's body either.

Papers and fliers with Wendy Von Huben's information was distributed all throughout Florida up through Illinois.

Authorities also began interviewing the transient population that lived along the railroad tracks.

Two and a half months later, however, Wendy's parents would receive a phone call.

"The phone rang," Rosenquest recalled. "Wendy's father answered the phone. The girl was crying. She said 'I'm sorry. I love you.'"

She would tell the father she was two hours away from Woodstock at a gas station. The father asked for the phone number on the pay phone she was calling from and she said that there wasn't any before hanging up.

The police were not certain that the phone call came from Wendy so they immediately headed out to the gas station where they believe the call took place.

Police tracked down the surveillance video of the gas station. On the video, a woman that physically resembled Wendy entered the gas station.

The phone records, however, revealed that the call did not come from the gas station where the surveillance video revealed a woman who allegedly was Wendy. It came from another gas station where there were fliers posted of Wendy.

Someone had played a cruel hoax as Wendy's parents had added their home number to the fliers

ONE-LEGGED BOB AND A CHANCE DISCOVERY

A year went by without any sign of Wendy.

There was some ray of hope, however, as the railroad authorities called the Ocala police and informed them that the received information from a member of one of the homeless camps. They had a man in custody named "One Legged Bob" who was traveling with a girl and may be responsible for the murder of her previous boyfriend.

"'One Legged Bob' was your typical homeless person," Owens said. "Kinda scruffy. Hadn't shaved in a few days. He had a prosthetic leg that helped him get around. For someone who you might consider crippled, he was far from crippled."

Owens would spend the next eight hours interviewing the only lead he had, a one legged homeless man.

After the grueling interrogation, Owens realized that he had the wrong suspect.

By sheer chance, however, Patty Lumpkin heard about someone they dubbed the "Railroad Killer" during a class she was taking at the FBI.

"They called him the Railway Killer," Lumpkin recalled. "The Angel of Death. He was killing people. Leaving them near the railroad or he was killing them at homes or locations that were close to the railroad.

The FBI knew the Railway Killer as Angel Resendiz.

"We knew that Angel Resendiz was a person that rode the rails across the country," FBI Agent Mark Young said. "We were worried where he'd wind up next. So we decided to make him a top ten fugitive. Maybe the millions of eyes of the public would tell us something."

The strategy worked.

"He was one of the most vile, evil persons that I had ever dealt with," Young said. "It was like every time you turn around there's another murder."

Owens and Lumpkin hoped to talk to Resendiz to query him about Jesse Howell's murder and Wendy Von Huben's disappearance.

"The attorneys representing him at the time in Texas stopped us," Owens said. "They wanted to protect their client from talking. Any defense attorney who represents a criminal will generally tell the person to stop talking to law enforcement."

Resendiz was placed on death row and Texas had a fast execution rate. The two detectives worried that they would lose their chance to interview Resendiz and connect him to the crimes in Ocala.

Owens and Lumpkin decided to mail Resendiz a letter, respectfully asking him if they could interview him. The letter was written in a formal manner and even addressed him as "Senor."

To their surprise, Resendiz responded back and granted them an interview regarding his involvement in Jesse's killing and Wendy's disappearance.

During their meeting, Resendiz was quick to admit that he had killed Jesse. The detectives deliberately withheld information about the killing, holding back details that only the killer would know. But when Resendiz described using a brake coupling from one of the trains, they knew they had their killer.

But they needed to find out what happened to Wendy.

In a follow-up letter, they promised him immunity from prosecution if he agreed to talk. It was a moot point by then as he was already on death row but the detectives still needed permission from Wendy's family to go through with the interview.

In order to receive some sense of closure, the family agreed to the immunity.

"When we get to the prison," Lumpkin said. "We see him coming down the hallway. He (Resendiz) has a waist belt on. It's an electric shock belt and he's chained to the belt. He's just a mild-mannered person but remember that a psychopath or a sociopath doesn't have any feeling. I mean he had dead eyes. He had no feeling in that body. He didn't care about anything."

Resendiz would reveal that he was heading south for work when the train stopped and he spotted Jesse getting off the train for a smoke.

"Resendiz told us that he killed Jesse with a piece of the train coupling," Lumpkin said. "And Wendy was asleep on the train when this took place. And then when they went down the road further somehow he talked Wendy into getting off the train."

Resendiz then raped and strangled Wendy to death.

Resendiz drew a map of where had left Wendy's body. He described burying her in a shallow grave near a canopy of trees. Resendiz would remember that she had a book in a back pack and an army style jacket that he used to cover her fresh grave.

Police would return to the site and were able to locate where he buried Wendy's body. Almost three years after the murder, everything the killer described was still there. The book. The jacket.

And Wendy's body.

"When Wendy ran away she had a small engagement ring," Owen said. "And she had a Winnie the Pooh wristwatch.

The detective would bring those items back to Wendy's parents.

KENTUCKY RAILROAD MURDER

In August of 1997, Resendiz would make his way from Ocala, Florida to Lexington, Kentucky. It was there he would stalk two young college students.

Holly Dunn was a 20-year old junior at the University of Kentucky and it was there she met Christopher Maier.

"Chris Maier was my very good friend," Dunn recalled. "He was just the nicest, kindest man. We decided that we wanted to be more than friends then we started dating. We dated for about three months."

"Chris and I were attending a party. We decided that the party wasn't very fun so we went to go talk a walk by the railroad tracks. We sat down and talked for awhile and when we got up to leave a man came out from behind an electrical box. He had a weapon that he used on Chris. It was some sort of ice pick or screw driver. Something sharp. I guess our immediate thought was he's going to rob us. That's when we realize he wants money we start thinking 'okay, well, you could have our credit card, you can have our ATM card, you can have our car.' Then he started tying up Chris' hands behind his back. And then he came over to me and he took off my belt and that's when I started thinking he doesn't want to rob us."

After tying up Holly, Resendiz then pulled Chris by the shirt across the railroad tracks and into a ditch.

Holly would follow on her knees, pleading for him to stop whatever he was about to do.

"Lie down," Resendiz said, his voice soft but menacing.

"Everything is going to be okay," Christopher said to Holly as Resendiz dragged him into the ditch.

"Shut up!" Resendiz commanded as he gagged Christopher with a sock.

Resendiz then walked off into the darkness. The frightened couple did not know what the psychopath had planned.

"Then he comes with this rock," Holly recalled. "There was no warning, he drops this rock on Chris' head. I'm just thinking 'what just happened?' I don't even know what just happened."

"You don't have to worry about him anymore," Resendiz said to Holly as he got on top of her.

"I went into survival mode, I'm thinking, I mean he's gonna kill me. I may as well fight. I'm gonna fight. He unties my feet and climbs on top of me. I start to kick and scream and hit him but he held that knife or ice pick (to my throat) and said 'look how easily I could kill you.' I stopped everything and then he raped me."

"I memorized his face," Dunn said. "I stared at him and memorized, he had a tattoo on his arm, I was thinking if you have any scars I'm gonna remember your scars, I'm gonna remember your face,I'm not gonna forget it because if I live through this I will get you."

Resendiz completed the sexual assault of Dunn before smashing her head with a rock.

"He hit me five or six times in my face," Dunn recalled. "I think I put my hand up and then I turned over and then he hit me five or six times in the back of my head. He hit me hard. He was trying to kill me. I think I laid there and he thought I was dead."

Resendiz did think she was did as he threw the rock down and ran away from the crime scene.

Holly would suffer severe facial trauma but miraculously survived the attack.

"I had a broken jaw," Dunn said. "Broken eye socket and cuts on the back of my head that they had to staple shut and then I had cuts on my face."

She woke up in a Kentucky hospital, surrounded by family members.

"Everyone was told not to talk about Chris to me. I just said 'Chris is dead, isn't he?' And my Dad actually is the one I said that to and he was like 'yes, he died.'"

TEXAS TERROR

Resendiz would travel to Texas via train and in October of 1988 he flopped down in Hughes Springs. He would enter the home of 87-year old Leafie Mason, attacking the woman with an iron and killing her.

Two months later, Resendiz would sneak into the home of Dr. Claudia Benton, a thirty-nine year old medical researcher who lived in a suburb of Houston near the railroad tracks.

Again, it was a case of a home being to close to the train tracks. The train would provide the perfect cover for the sneaky Resendiz as he realized that the sound of the rail-car racing by would allow him to break in homes without being heard.

He applied the same technique with Benton, breaking into her home, raping then killing her.

Police would find the doctor face down on the floor. Her bedroom soaked in blood, ransacked for any valuables.

He head had been covered in a plastic bag while her body had been covered in a blanket.

"It appears that she (Claudia Benton) was sleeping," recalled Ken Macha, former police sergeant. "He was able to get in and picked up a bronze statuette from the mantle in the living room. He was relentless in beating her. The skull fractures themselves would have been enough to kill her. She was then stabbed in the back with a very large butcher knife."

"Resendiz was brutal, sadistic," said former West University police chief Gary Brye.

Fingerprints and DNA evidence would link Resendiz to the crime.

The problem was they could catch the man that Texas Ranger Drew Carter referred to as "a walking, breathing form of evil."

EVADING POLICE

Seven months later, Resendiz would continue to avoid capture. He remained in Texas, riding the rail cars until coming into the town of Weimar. He would break into the home of Pastor Norman "Skip" Sirnic and his wife Karen. Resendiz smashed a jack hammer into both of their heads, killing them instantly. He would then rape the body of Karen postmortem.

"He would watch these places," prosecuting attorney Devin Anderson said. "He would watch them, wait for them to go to sleep, get in their house and he would strike them before they would even wake up. I thought we have got to catch this guy."

The DNA found at the scene of the Sirnic murders would match those left on Benton. The FBI then realized they had a highly mobile serial killer on the loose...someone who could kill in one town then appear in another town miles away and kill again.

Resendiz was also smart. He would constantly alter his appearance. He'd shave his head. Then his mustache. He'd be clean shaven one week. Unkempt the next. He would wear glasses one week. No glasses the next.

Authorities could not get an accurate description of him other than the fact that he was small.

Resendiz was also able to take advantage of the lack of a coordinated computer system that gave law enforcement the ability to cross-check fugitives. After the Sirnic murders, Border Patrol had encountered Resendiz near the El Paso border but did not find him on the wanted list.

They then deported him back to Mexico.

Within 48 hours, Resendiz was back across the border to resume his killing spree.

"Our computers told us that he was nothing of lookout material," said C.G. Almengor, a supervisor at the border."We really wish he had been in the system so we could have caught him."

Resendiz would be deported no less than seventeen times over the course of his rampage. At no point did authorities make the connection because of his changing appearance, use of different aliases and the lack of a connected system to document illegals trying to come across the border.

A PREFERENCE FOR TEXAS

Noemi Dominguez was a graduate of Rice University who had just recently quit her job as an elementary school teacher to pursue a master's degree.

She was described as "the sweetest, nicest teacher – a darling who went the extra mile."

Fueled by hate, Resendiz would break into Noemi's home and rape her before killing her with a pick ax. He then stole her car and drove to Schulenberg, Texas where he would kill Josephine Konvicka with the same pick ax.

He would leave the weapon embedded in Konvicka's head as well as leave his fingerprints all over the home. He was more than just sloppy, he was getting cocky. He left a newspaper article that described his crimes as well as a toy train...a reference to his nickname as the "Railroad Killer."

Resendiz was also meticulous in approaching his victims.

"He undid the light in her (Noemi's) car," Anderson said. "So when he opened the door it wouldn't come on. That's who were were dealing with. Someone who really knew how to sneak around. Who really knew how to avoid detection."

"He kept killing people. He would not stop. In his mode of transportation, using the railroads was brilliant because they couldn't be monitored. I mean there's thousands of trains and millions of miles of tracks all over the United States."

"I felt hopeless at the time. Because if you're willing to sleep in a train or you're willing to sleep in a field, you can stay lost for a long, long time and I didn't think we were ever going to catch him."

Later that month, Resendiz had journeyed to Illinois, reaching the town of Gorham. He would break into the home of 80-year old George Morber and his daughter Carolyn Frederick. Resendiz would tie Morber to a chair and shoot him in the back of the head with a shotgun. He then raped Carolyn and smashed the shotgun across her head with such force that the weapon broke in half.

Both Morber and Frederick would die from their injuries.

The FBI placed him on their Top Ten list.

They then recruited his common-law wife, Julietta Reyes, and brought her into Houston for questioning from her hometown of Rodeo, Mexico.

Reyes complied with police requests, turning over over ninety-three pieces of jewelry that her husband had mailed to her from the U.S.

Relatives of Noemi Dominguez claimed thirteen pieces. George Benton was able to identify some pieces of jewelry as belonging to his wife as well.

Police would then locate Resendiz's half-sister, Manuela Karkiewicz, who lived in New Mexico. Initially, she refused to cooperate. She worried that the FBI or the police would kill her brother. But Carter convinced her to talk Resendiz into giving himself up.

The FBI knew that Resendiz had made his way back to Mexico after the murders in Illinois and was hiding in his hometown neighborhood of Patria.

Carter was able to get a rapport with Manuela. He convinced her that Resendiz would receive "personal safety while in jail, regular visiting rights for his family and a psychological evaluation."

"I came away with the impression that they (Resendiz' family) definitely had an understanding of right and wrong ... and knew now that what Maturino Resendiz was accused of doing was heinous and wrong ... ," Carter said. "Manuela, especially, came across as a woman of strong faith. There was a very deep emotional strain and burden placed on her in this investigation. She had to make some very difficult choices that impacted her and her family. And, in the end, her actions alone speak to her character."

Carter spent weeks talking to Manuela who in turn "worked a miracle."

They got the serial killer to surrender.

On July 12th, Manuela would receive a fax from the district attorney's office in Harris County which formalized everything that Texas Ranger Carter had promised.

The word passed from Manuela to another relative who acted as a go-between with Resendiz. The relative than came back later that evening and said that Resendiz would surrender in the morning at 9 a.m.

Texas Ranger Drew Carter would accompany Manuela and a spiritual adviser to meet with Resendiz on a bridge that connected El Paso, Texas to Ciudad Juarez.

"When I saw that face there was a little bit of excitement there because I finally said, 'This is going to happen,'" Carter recalled as he remembered Resendiz appearing on the bridge with his dirty jeans, muddy boots and blank facial expression. "He stuck out his hand, I stuck out my hand, and we shook hands."

Resendiz would then surrender to the Texas Ranger.

DEATH PENALTY

Resendiz' attorneys knew that their only hope would be an insanity defense. The Mexican government also got involved, lobbying authorities to spare Resendiz the death penalty

"Insanity was the logical defense because no one wants to believe that there is someone out there who would do things like that," Anderson said. "That was the thing that worried me the most about the case was that jurors would just throw up their hands and say nobody in their right mind could do what he does."

"The thing about what a life sentence with Resendiz would have been, he would have enjoyed it. I mean he would have had pen pals. He would have given interviews if they let him, I mean he would have loved it. And I knew that. And he didn't deserve to live after what he did just didn't. He caused so much pain, so much heartache and so much terror, that's what the whole focus of the trial had to be."

George Benton, the husband of Claudia, would vehemently criticize the Mexican government who support his appeals and domestic opposition to the death penalty.

"(He)looked like a man and walked like a man. But what lived within that skin was not a human being."

"He was small," Anderson said when she first saw Resendiz in the courtroom. "Maybe five- foot five. His forearms though, were roped with muscles. He was scary. Even though he was small you could feel he was dangerous. He looked like a wild animal who'd been caught."

Resendiz looked "timid" in the courtroom and spoke of himself in religious riddles. He claimed he was Jewish and didn't seem effected when he was informed that the prosecution was aiming for the death penalty.

"I don't believe in death," Resendiz, said. "I know the body is going to go to waste. But me, as a person, I'm eternal. I'm going to be alive forever."

The defense said that Resendiz' crimes were caused by head injuries, drug abuse and a family history of mental illness. He has a delusional perception of the world as he believes that he can cause earthquakes, floods, and explosions and that God told him to kill his victims whom they believed to be evil.

He made a living stealing things from his victims and having his wife sell them in Mexico. "That was his job," Anderson said. "And for recreation it was killing the people who lived in the house."

"He was a very intelligent person who worked the system and knew exactly what kinds of things to say to get that defense to work."

The jury, however, would find Resendiz guilty after one hour and forty-five minutes of deliberation.

He was sentenced to die via lethal injection.

"He made it very clear during my conversation with him that he deserves to die," Owens said.

"I want to ask if it is in your heart to forgive me," Resendiz said in his final words. "You don't have to. I know I allowed the devil to rule my life. I just ask you to forgive me and ask the Lord to forgive me for allowing the devil to deceive me. I thank God for having patience with me. I don't deserve to cause you pain. You did not deserve this. I deserve what I am getting."

Resendiz then prayed in Hebrew and Spanish before drawing his final breath.

THE CAMDEN RIPPER

DWIGHT HALL

Whitechapel, London was not a safe place for women in the 1880's, as an unknown man was killing prostitutes throughout the region, and police had no idea who this mystery person was. He was eventually dubbed 'Jack the Ripper', but his real identity was never discovered. Just over a hundred years later London became precarious once again as Anthony Hardy, a man who has been obsessed with Jack the Ripper for most of his life, took to the streets to emulate his hero. Hardy was eventually given the name 'the Camden Ripper', but this time, police are on to his game.

Anthony Hardy was born on May 31, 1951, to parents in a working-class suburb of London. His father was a miner and worked hard to support his wife and five children. According to many, Hardy's childhood in Burton upon Trent was unremarkable.

"He seems to have been an uncomplicated child. A bit quiet, a bit of a loner," said Dr. Jane Monkton Smith, criminologist

Often times, experts point to a traumatic event in childhood to explain a serial killer's motives for becoming so twisted, but Hardy experienced nothing traumatic growing up, the only negative in his life was his embarrassment at being born into a lower class family.

Hardy was a remarkably bright child. He excelled in school. Although he was expected to follow in his father's footsteps and become a miner, Hardy had bigger, more important dreams for himself.

"His father was a miner and they were from the lower middle class, which he didn't like," said Smith.

Nigel Weir, senior police detective, explained why Hardy was so desperate to separate himself from his low-class family; "it was normal that you would follow your father, so it was expected that Anthony would go down the mines. He obviously wanted to choose something better for himself."

Hardy worked hard to improve his prospects. After he finished primary and high school, Hardy went on to attend Imperial College in London, a very prestigious school where he studied engineering.

Hardy's intelligence would later become a key characteristic, and would shape the unspeakable crimes he would commit as an adult.

Even at this young age, Hardy was beginning to believe few people, if any, could match his level of intelligence.

Weir explained Hardy's internal thoughts at this time as, " 'I'm cleverer than you,' that is what would come out of this, because at the end of the day, academically, he was cleverer," said Weir.

Throughout college Hardy continued to distinguish himself as a bright individual. He soon realized he also had a way with the women on campus, who were attracted to his brains and his looks.

In 1972, while he was still attending school, Hardy married Judith Dwight. She was his equal in both intelligence and looks, and from the outside, it seemed as if the two were a perfect match.

"She was obviously his equal in terms of intellectual achievement and understanding, and they appeared a fine match," said Colin Sutton, metropolitan police officer.

Once he graduated from college, Hardy began working for British Sugar. It was a prestigious job and one which helped Hardy move out of the lower class once and for all, or so he thought.

Things were good for the young couple, so they decided it was time to start a family, and soon four children were born. Happiness didn't last long for the Hardy's however. The stress of such a high profile job was hard on Hardy, and the rest of the family and Hardy began to show a violent nature towards his wife.

"What I think is pretty clear looking at the history of their relationship, that it wasn't just a little bit of domestic violence," said Smith. "Anthony Hardy was pretty much what we would call a stereotypical abuser."

Sutton also offers a chilling detail about Hardy's inclination towards violence, "the predisposition to extreme violence will often be accompanied by a willingness to use violence against your loved ones," he said.

Looking back, it's hard not to wonder if authorities had noticed the violence early in Hardy's life, could they have stopped this man from becoming the horrifying killer known as the Camden Ripper?

As well as becoming habitually violent, Hardy began traveling with his job around this time, and established a lifelong addiction to sex, anyway, he could get it. He began to have a number of extramarital affairs with prostitutes. He didn't even try to hide the secret from his wife, or anyone else. Hardy's hero, Jack the Ripper was known for having relationships with prostitutes as well.

"A number of prostitutes came forward to say they had encountered him," said Steve Bird, crime reporter. "A lot of them gave harrowing accounts of how violent he was during the sex act. Some of them said they were unable to breathe while he had sex with them. Others claimed that he was just incredibly violent and seemed to be into sadomasochism."

In the mid-1970's life is not great for the Hardy family, but things are about to get worse, the working class boy who had worked hard to transform his fortunes lost his job. It's not his fault, just an economic downturn. But, Hardy begins to suffer from depression and mood swings and doctors prescribed him medication. Today he would be diagnosed as bipolar, a condition still uncategorized at the time, and one which can lead to exceptionally violent behavior. The diagnosis is the start of a mental illness which will shape his life forever, and end the lives of others he encounters along the way.

Instead of going down in the mines, Hardy took a job halfway across the world in Tasmania, Australia in the late 1970's. It should have been a fresh start for the family, but instead, things only got worse from there.

"The family was very excited about the move to Tasmania, it sounds very exotic, a place where the family could consider themselves starting fresh," said Bird.

If the family was hoping for a fresh start in a new place, they were sadly mistaken, Hardy's desire for sex outside of his marriage was just as strong as it was in London. It was later established while in Tasmania Hardy still had affairs, still visited prostitutes, still abused his wife. He became more controlling over every aspect of his life.

"The group of men who are particularly dangerous, and the group of men who serially commit domestic violence are usually incredibly controlling individuals," said Smith, "and Anthony Hardy was one of those individuals."

Hardy was not able to keep his new job for long. In 1986, for the second time, Hardy was let go in a round of job cuts.

As Hardy's life spun even more out of control, he became more violent. Hardy's marriage wasn't working, he was clinically depressed, and had yet again been thrown out of a job. Throughout this time, he had maintained a fascination with Jack the Ripper. He read books about the mysterious killer on a regular basis. But, while the 19th-century slaughterer used crude methods to kill, Hardy chose a more devious means for his first attempt at murder. The victim, his wife.

"He tried to create a perfect crime," said Bird. "He actually used his scientific knowledge to be able to carry out a crime that he hoped would be undetectable."

Hardy filled a water bottle full of water and then froze it. As the bottle was freezing, Hardy drew a bath. Once everything was ready, Hardy took the frozen water bottle from his freezer and went to find his sleeping wife. He beat her over the head repeatedly with the bottle. Once she was severely injured, and semi-conscious, Hardy planned to put her in the bathtub. Later, when the authorities found her, Hardy assumed they would rule her death an accidental drowning because it would look as if she had been knocked unconscious after slipping while entering the tub. In the meantime, his murder weapon would melt, and he could dispose of all the evidence. Hardy thought he would never be discovered, just like his hero, Jack the Ripper.

"The amount of planning is quite unusual, that he would plan that far in advance," said Smith.

One thing Hardy didn't count on in his plan was his wife making noise as he was beating her. She was so loud, she woke up their young children at one point, who came into the room to see what was going on. The authorities were called before any serious damage could be done, and Judith escaped from certain death.

"Hardy didn't care the effect it [his attack] had on his child, it was just part and parcel of him getting his own way," said Bird.

Hardy was arrested after the attack on his wife, but he wasn't worried.

"He confessed to it and said he had actually fully intended to kill her that night. This was a very, very dangerous man," said Smith.

Anthony Hardy had exhibited a taste for the sort of brutality used by Jack the Ripper. He now faced jail time for attempted murder. But, this was in an era when domestic violence was dealt with differently than today, and his crime was considered just that, domestic violence.

"Their view was in 1970's Australia, the same as 1970's England; it's a domestic, it stays at home," said Weir.

Hardy knew he was smarter than any police officer, and he would be able to talk his way out of this situation. He soon convinced the police he was mentally unstable and he didn't need jail time, he needed to spend time in a mental hospital until he could recover his senses. The police agreed and he was sent to a hospital to be evaluated by psychologists.

Hardy told a friend, Maureen Reeves, years later going into the mental hospital was all an act to fool people for whom he had no respect.

"He said that, 'they're not very intelligent because they couldn't catch Jack the Ripper.' " Reeves said. "With the psychologists, he said, 'they're not very clever people.' And I said, 'well they must be because that's their job, you know, to help people.' He said, 'no, you can tell them things and they sometimes just agree with you.' But he always said he could beat a psychologist."

Inside the psychiatric unit in Queensland Hardy cooperated with staff, he took his medication, he played the game with just one intention, to get out as quickly as possible.

"He evaded, what otherwise would have been perhaps a pretty stiff sentence for a crime of attempted murder," said Sutton.

After a few months in the hospital, Hardy was released. His family had returned to England while he was away, but because this is still the 1970's there is no restraining order in place, and Hardy was free to go back to England himself and stalk them.

"Even though he had tried to kill his wife, he returned to Britain an innocent man," said Smith.

After his release from the hospital, Hardy became even more dangerous.

"It's possible that Mr. Hardy believed that being released back into normal life, then he's beaten the system," said Weir. "He beat the police in Australia. As far as he's concerned, he's back. He's number one."

Judith called the police several times to report her ex-husband following her, but there is little that can be done to stop it.

"She would regularly contact police saying this guy was still after her," said Bird, "and he became increasingly sinister, increasingly menacing towards her."

It's around this time Hardy begins a normal friendship with Reeves. He keeps his dark past hidden from her, and she has no reason to suspect Hardy is hiding anything sinister, nor does she have any idea of the horrors her new friend will commit in the future. Hardy even talks to Reeves sometimes about his obsession with Jack the Ripper, but still, she doesn't think anything is out of the ordinary.

"No other person for ten years knew him how I knew him, and all the discussions we had about different things, alright yes he was obsessed with Jack the Ripper, but that to me is not unusual, some people are interested, some people are fascinated by him," said Reeves.

The family of Anthony Hardy is tormented for several months, Hardy himself becomes more intense with his threats and actions towards the family. Finally, Judith is able to get a restraining order put in place for her ex-husband. But, his need to control her is too great. He broke the restraining order and was punished with a short jail sentence.

"Stalkers are very often obsessive people," said Sutton. "Of course, obsessions can lead to behavior which is out of the ordinary and not what one would expect."

On his release from jail, Hardy decides to finally leave his old family alone. He moved on to easier and more vulnerable targets; prostitutes. Hardy moved to the Kings Cross area of London. Near Whitechapel, where it was just over a century before where Hardy's hero Jack the Ripper terrorized the streets and killed without mercy.

"Kings Cross at the time attracted a transient population, there was a major train station there," said Bird. "It was where prostitutes, pimps and drug dealers hanged out. For Hardy, this was an ideal place to live."

It seemed as if Hardy was given a fresh start in Kings Cross. The police in this area were not aware of his violent past, or the fact he had tried to kill his wife when they were living in Australia. To them, he was just another man obsessed with sex taking full advantage of what the prostitutes were offering in this area. Unfortunately, no one has any idea just how much danger these women are in.

"That's when you see a deterioration in not only the quality of his life but also in the quality of his mental state," said Sutton. "There seems to have been a spiral of deterioration involving drugs, involving alcohol and depression which lead him to the low point until the horror that we ultimately saw."

In the late 1990's Hardy was diagnosed with diabetes, a condition in which, in his case, caused impotence. This could have been the final straw to push this once high achiever to multiple murderer. Although he was now impotent, Hardy was still just as addicted to sex as before, so he began to seek out more devious, and more violent sex to satisfy his needs.

"For a man who's already violent, who already suffers rages perhaps, and who is already a misogynist, to then find that he cannot achieve satisfaction in the usual ways and has to go further and further that's going to be a problem," said Smith.

Anthony Hardy was now set on a road to destruction. The consequences seemed inevitable.

"He is a sadistic and controlling individual. He suffers with psychotic incidences," said Smith. "So, we've got a man who is not totally in control and who is, to put it in simple terms, a ticking time bomb."

The bomb is about to explode. Hardy was now living in a run-down area of London, filled with prostitutes, and degradation. He craved sex and drugs, and both were easy enough to get. His life, which once seemed so bright and full of promise was now in ruins and Hardy didn't seem to care. He would go for long periods of time without washing himself, or even changing his clothes. Hardy only had one thing on his mind now; violence. And he won't stop till get gets it.

Hardy still cultivates relationships with vulnerable prostitutes as often as he can, the encounters are just as violent as ever. In 1998, he went too far and a prostitute accused him of rape. How can Hardy escape justice this time?

"These crimes sometimes being difficult to prove, and certainly in 1998, and sometimes victims being unwilling to go through with it because the support perhaps wasn't there for them at the time," said Sutton. "It came to nothing in terms of the prosecution, but it came, we have a very serious indication, precursor, of how Hardy was prepared to treat women."

After the accusation, Hardy was arrested and questioned by the police. He was soon released, however, due to lack of evidence, and because the prostitute in question did not wish to testify in court. Once again, Hardy escaped justice. Once again, Hardy thought he was above the law. And once again, Hardy thought he was untouchable.

"He's thinking, 'I'm untouchable, I'm unalike, they're not going to get me,'" said Sutton.

It was around this time Hardy struck up a friendship with one of his neighbors, Alan Young. The two met in the courtyard of their apartment building and soon began chatting. Young had no idea just how dangerous the person he was talking to would turn out to be.

"We just had conversations, that's all. Just everyday topics, things like that, a bit of politics, bits of this that and the other. And that was it," said Young of how the two first met.

Hardy was careful not to reveal too much to his new friend and kept his darkest secrets deep inside.

The next few years passed in relative normalcy, but Hardy did not get along with all his neighbors as well as he did with Young. In 2002, the police were called to the apartment complex after a dispute between Hardy and one such neighbor got out of hand. To get back at a neighbor for her shower or bath supposedly dripping water in Hardy's apartment, he defaced her door with several obscenities, then he threw battery acid through her mail slot.

"It wasn't just simple criminal damage, this was really rather nasty abuse across the door and battery acid through the mail slot," said Smith. "They already knew that they were dealing with somebody who was potentially quite dangerous."

As police were investigating the incident they noticed a door in Hardy's apartment which was locked. They asked him for the key, and he responded by saying he didn't have one. The room was, according to Hardy, used by a border and he did not have access.

Police didn't question Hardy's story, but they asked him to grab a jacket and come with them down to the police station for further questioning. One quick look in the pockets of the jacket Hardy grabbed, and police found the key to open this door. What the police found behind the door was more shocking than they could ever have imagined.

"What they found then was obviously quite horrific for anybody to find," said Weir. "They found, lying on the bed, the naked body of a woman. We're thinking the worst, we're thinking suspicious, we're thinking has he killed this woman."

Earlier in the week, a sex worker named Sally Rose White had come into contact with Hardy while she was working the streets. Her colleagues would never see her again, they had no idea where she disappeared to after she was seen with Hardy, but they did know she was in great danger. White was born with a spinal injury which plagued her for most of her life, with both physical and mental disabilities. It was difficult for her to hold down any job, besides prostitution, and her drug addiction left her with no other choice. It was her body police stumbled upon when they opened the locked door in Hardy's apartment. She was dead.

"It must be quite a horrific thing to realize they were encountering a body, and probably had in their midst a murder," said Bird.

On the walls of the room where White's body was found there were satanic markings, there was photography equipment throughout the room, and there was a pile of pornographic videos on a table as well. White was positioned on a bed; her body was arranged as if she were taking part in a twisted macabre photo shoot. White had suffered head and neck injuries and there was a bite mark on her leg.

In 1888, Jack the Ripper had created a similar scene with one of his murder victims laid out on a bed. Hardy was once again emulating his hero.

Smith believed this was how Hardy now reached sexual satisfaction.

"Anthony Hardy was unable to get sexual satisfaction from ordinary sex," said Smith. "He himself had complained that it was making him very frustrated and very, very angry. It was something that he couldn't control. The sadism started to go up. The act of killing women actually provided him with some satisfaction sexually."

Hardy told police he had no idea this woman was in his apartment, let alone dead. But, there was a bucket of soapy water in the room, and it was still warm. Police wondered if Hardy had just been using the water to wash away a bloody mess.

As police began to piece together this horrific crime, it looked as if Hardy was finally caught. He was taken down to the station for a complete investigation and police believed he would be put behind bars for life. What happened next, nobody expected. A home office pathologist, who was later fired for incompetence, was sent to examine the body, he ruled the woman had died from natural causes. Hardy was once again off the hook.

"The police must have been infuriated when a coroner rules someone who is found naked with a smack to the back of her head," said Bird. "They must have been absolutely astonished that a coroner would say this was natural causes. I mean to them, they must have been convinced this girl died from a heart attack through fear."

"Had Sally been completely healthy from birth, and not had these difficulties, then it might have been that the decision that she had died from natural causes wouldn't have been so easy to come to," said Sutton.

Once it was ruled White had died from natural causes, and not murder, the rest of the evidence ceased to matter, the position she was found in, the photographic equipment, even the fact that she was found in a man's apartment she hardly knew didn't matter anymore. The investigation was finished. Hardy had once again beaten the police. Further supporting his belief, he was to live out the same fate as Jack the Ripper.

When Hardy was released from jail, he returned to his apartment and talked to Young as if nothing had happened.

"I didn't say nothing, funnily enough, he said it, 'oh I suppose you saw me in the paper.' I said, 'Tony, yeah I did.' He said, 'do you believe I didn't do it?' I said, 'Tony if you say so. Who am I to call you a liar?' And that was it. And that was all Tony said," Young said.

Although he had escaped the charge of murder, Hardy was still charged with the crime of defacing his neighbors' door. But, it was a relatively minor crime comparatively. To escape jail time, Hardy used his mental illness and convinced authorities what he really needed was treatment in a mental hospital, not a jail sentence. They agreed, and Hardy was sent for the second time in his life to a hospital instead of a jail.

"He used his mental illnesses as a smoke screen. To try and evade detection, to try and justify who he was and how he behaved," said Bird.

While in the hospital, Hardy was compliant, pleasant and good natured, once again he thought this behavior would fool the doctors and he would soon be released.

"It came to November of 2002, and there was a panel that could meet, an administrative panel, to decide on his future. And although the medical professionals would still say; 'he should stay, he should remain,' the panel came to the decision that he could be released," said Sutton.

To the outside world, it looked as if the treatment had been a success. Hardy was safe once again to enter the normal population. This time, Hardy would commit the crimes which will make him infamous, and synonymous with his long-time hero Jack the Ripper.

Hardy went back to abusing drugs, sex and pornography almost as soon as he was released. He craved more violent sex and did anything he could to get it. He wrote letters to all the prostitutes he had known in the past, trying to get them to spend another night with him.

Shortly before Christmas of 2002, Hardy meet a young prostitute named Elizabeth Valad. It was easy enough for him to convince her to come to his apartment with the promise of drugs. It would be her last day alive. Valad had fallen in with the bad crowd in high school, and after she graduated she moved into her own place, telling her family she was working as a secretary, but really working the streets. When her family found out, they tried to bring her back home, but she refused. Once she met Hardy, no one could save her from her fate.

"We know that they did indulge in extreme sex and bondage which ended with Elizabeth being strangled," said Smith. "She was then posed sexually, a devil mask, devil iconography. She was posed and photographed, which is apparently how Anthony Hardy achieved satisfaction," she added.

Weir explained Hardy's seemingly unusual fascination with taking pictures of his victims in this way; "Mr. Hardy committed a crime and took a picture of that almost as if he was proud to have committed the crime and photographed it. Some killers do respond like that. It's his work, he's proud of his work," he said.

Hardy gave the negatives of these photos to a friend for safekeeping. He had no idea he had just been given evidence of his friend's grizzly past-time.

Not long after, Hardy meets another young sex worker, Brigette MacClennan. MacClennan had a normal enough life until her marriage broke up in the early 1990's, she soon turned to drugs to ease her pain, and quickly found the only way to support her habit was to sell herself on the street. She was soon persuaded to go back to Hardy's home, where she met the same unspeakable fate as Elizabeth had just days earlier.

"Once again, the object of murder seems to have been taking these photographs," said Sutton. "There were those photographs of Bridget in similar poses to those found in relation to Elizabeth."

Smith also had an idea as to why Hardy was attacking these young women.

"He appeared to be using devil worshiping iconography, but the ritual would be more how he would achieve sexual satisfaction. That was the ritual element to this I think, and the posing of the bodies really reveals where his sexual depravities were," she said.

Two dead women were now in Hardy's apartment. Neighbors and close friends had no idea what had been going on in the building, but soon they would hear the sounds of what they assumed to be late night home improvements. Still, no one was suspicious. Hardy had planned for this event, and everything was in place. He had acquired both a hand saw and an electric power saw, and he put gloves on before he began his gruesome task. He dismembered and cut up both of the women. Once they had been cut into small enough pieces he put the remains in garbage bags and took them to a dumpster close by.

"Dismemberment is quite a horrific act. The ability to be able to do it, suggests someone who is utterly cold and calculating," said Bird.

Hardy did not seem bothered by the gruesome task he just completed, and he didn't even take care to put the remains in a trash can a greater distance from where the murders took place. The trash cans were even monitored by CCTV cameras, Hardy was well aware of this fact, and at one point, as he was walking away from the disposing of a body, he gives the camera a look, as if acknowledging its presence.

"I mean he'd already effectively got away with a crime many months earlier with the discovery of the naked body. Perhaps he was teasing people. Perhaps he was teasing the police. 'Come and get me, I'll beat you again,' " said Weir.

Hardy was convinced he was just as untouchable as Jack the Ripper was.

On New Year's Eve 2002, four weeks after the death of Valard, a homeless man was rummaging through the trash cans trying to find some scraps to eat. He felt what he thought was salmon someone had tossed out, and took it out of the can to see if anything was salvageable for him to eat. What he found when he pulled his hand out is inconceivable. It was not salmon at all, but the remains of a human leg. A leg that once belonged to one of the prostitutes Hardy had lured back to his apartment. The man called the police and an investigation was quickly begun.

Fully aware of Hardy's past, he was immediately suspected. When police arrived at his apartment, Hardy was not there, but there was plenty of evidence to connect him to these crimes.

"They found a torso wrapped in bin liners, they found a saw with flesh on there," said Weir.

Hardy had fled the scene, but as police began to discover more about his grizzly past, Hardy was finally given the moniker he wanted all along, the press dubbed him 'the Camden Ripper', after his long-time hero. Although Hardy now realized he was a wanted man, he didn't flee too far, he still needed medication to control his diabetes, and so all he did was shave off his beard and went about his business as usual.

Both Young and Reeves were shocked when they heard the news their old friend was wanted for murder.

"Never dreamed of it. No way, he didn't look like a mass murderer, or a mad ax killer or whatever you want to call him. He did not come across to me like that," said Young.

"I think I was angry, really angry that I knew somebody like that. And I can't understand, even to this day, how he could do it," Reeves added.

Hardy was soon captured, but many think even in this situation, he was still the one in control.

"I don't for one minute think Tony was caught by police. I honestly believe that Tony wanted to be caught," said Reeves.

When he was brought in for questioning, however, Hardy once again believed he would outsmart the police and get away with his crimes. Every question the police ask him was answered with a short, curt, 'no comment.'

"He wasn't trying to talk his way out. But he obviously thought that he was clever enough that he didn't have anything to say and let's see what the police can prove," said Sutton.

Much of the evidence against Hardy had been destroyed, and without Hardy's cooperation, police were having a hard time building a case.

"The hands and the heads of these bodies have never been found. The key identifying parts of the bodies. The rest of the parts of the bodies were dumped in such a haphazard fashion, almost as if he was testing the police," said Smith.

Hardy adamantly denied his involvement in either of the murders of which he was accused, but police eventually gathered enough evidence to go to trial anyway. On the day of his trial Hardy changed his mind and admitted not only to the two killings he was accused of, but a third as well, the murder of White, the woman found naked in his apartment months earlier. He was quickly given three life sentences, one for each of the three women he killed.

In 2012 a judge held up the ruling of three life sentences and also ordered no appeals could be made, Anthony Hardy was too dangerous a man to ever be allowed out of a jail cell again.

"He will never be released back into the community. He is seen as far too dangerous. And that's quite rare in fact, for a whole life tariff to be handed down," said Smith.

The mystery does not end there, though, although Hardy is behind bars, and admitted to three killings some wonder how many more he was responsible for. Several similar crimes were committed in this area of London, around the same time, and have never been solved. Is the Camden Ripper responsible for more death and dismemberment than he let on? No one knows for sure, just like no one knows the real identity of Hardy's idol and inspiration Jack the Ripper.

"The fact that he'd been able to get away effectively with all these things he was doing, or all the things we know about that he was doing, I've no doubt there was probably more to it, that he also got away with," said Sutton.

Hardy thought he was smarter than the police, and therefore would never be caught. His brazenness can be seen at several points throughout his life of violence and crime, but in the end, it wasn't smarts that saved Hardy from the police it was just lucky breaks. Once his luck ran out, it was only a matter of time before the Camden Ripper would be caught and made to pay for the crimes he had committed. Londoners can sleep just a little better now knowing this ripper is no longer out for blood.

SOUTHSIDE STRANGLER : The True Story of Timothy Spencer Wilson

126

NATALIE MARSHALL

Timothy Wilson Spencer has the distinction of being the first American serial killer to be convicted on the basis of DNA evidence—evidence that also exonerated a man who had been in prison after being wrongly convicted of committing one of Spencer's murders. A troubled adolescent from Arlington, Virginia, with a deep hatred of women, Spencer utilized his cat-burglar skills, strength, and agility to gain entry into his victims' homes, lay wait, and then bind, rape, torture, and murder them. In total, Spencer had been linked to five murders and at least nine rapes in both Richmond and Arlington, Virginia. He was convicted of the murders of four of his victims and sentenced to death. Spencer was ultimately executed in the electric chair on 27 April 1994.

Early Life

Timothy Wilson Spencer was born on 17 March 1962 in Arlington, Virginia, and raised in the Green Valley section of town which was known as a lower-income, tough, predominately Black neighborhood. His parents were hard workers and had attended college but had divorced when he and his younger brother Travis were young. Travis commented that their mom was the best mother ever who worked hard to support them and spent time with them.

As an adolescent he had become increasing rebellious, first getting into trouble at the age of nine and again at 12 for urinating and defecating in the school yard. He was a poor student but intelligent. In the professional literature Spencer would be classified as a life-course-persistent offender who began deviant behavior at a young age which continued throughout his life with escalating degrees of crime. He had been implicated and/or convicted of six prior burglaries (three as a juvenile) and three counts of trespassing before being arrested for burglary in 1984 for which he served three years in prison before being released to a halfway house in the Southside area that was a transitional residence for nonviolent offenders. Because Spencer's conviction was for burglary he was considered to be nonviolent even though the evidence would ultimately show that he was a deliberately violent rapist and murderer. While in the halfway house Spencer was a loner who ate at the end of the table away from others and even watched television away from the rest of the residents. He did speak to one woman who worked at the halfway house and worked on her car so that he could borrow it. Whereas among the house rules were that residents sign in and out every time they come and go and had to follow a curfew, this procedure was poorly supervised and enforced.

In an interview, Spencer's younger brother Travis reiterated his utter disbelief that his brother was capable of what he did. Burglaries and other property crimes he said he could accept but someone who displayed such anger toward and hatred of women and who wanted to control them as badly as Spencer did by the systematic torture and strangulation of his victims was too much for him to believe. He even mentioned one time in his childhood where he and a friend stole some candy from a local store and were brought home in a police car that his older brother told him to never become like him.

A big question that has remained since Spencer's execution was whether someone like him was the product of nature or nurture. Some forensic psychologists say that deviant sexual preferences are hard-wired and that when combined with certain other factors can lead to deviant and aggressive behavior. The literature suggests that predatory psychopaths suffer from atrophy of the parts of the brain responsible for moral decision-making and aggression control and whereas this may be genetically influenced, the right combination of such traits coupled with environmental influences can make someone commit heinous acts. Spencer exhibited some of the "classic" signs of the serial killer typology—bedwetting, cruelty to animals, and a propensity for setting fires—which facilitated the escalation of his actions from breaking and entering to arson to burglary to rape to murder.

The Crimes

Debbie Davis

Spencer's first reported victim was 35-year old Debbie Dudley Davis. On 18 September 1987 he entered her home through a kitchen window with a rocking chair below it and bound, raped, tortured, and murdered her. Detective Ray Williams—who was dispatched to this and each subsequent murder scene in Richmond and stated that he had never seen such disturbing crime scenes in his entire career—remarked that the intruder had to have been exceptionally strong and agile.

The assailant utilized materials found on the premises to fashion his homemade ratchet strangulation contraption and this would be a commonality at all his subsequent crime scenes. In this case, he utilized socks, shoelaces, and a 16-inch vacuum cleaner extension hose.

There was very little forensic evidence at the scene—no hair or fibers—and no witnesses which suggested that the assailant was very meticulous. Except for the semen.

Autopsy results on Davis suggested that she was murdered between 9:00 p.m. on Saturday, 18 September and 9:30 a.m. on Sunday, 19 September. At the time of her murder, Spencer lived 2.7 miles from her apartment which would be approximately a 37-minute walk. The halfway house log showed that he left at 7:30 p.m. on Friday and returned at 12:30 a.m. Saturday. Davis had spoken to her parents on the phone from 8:30 p.m. to 9:00 p.m. that Saturday evening.

She had been strangled with a sock and vacuum cleaner hose that the Virginia court said had been "fashioned into a ligature and ratchet-type device." According to the medical examiner, the contraption had been twisted two or three times, ultimately causing Davis' death. The pressure of the ligature was so strong, in fact, that her neck muscles, larynx, and voice box were cut; blood was congested within her head; one of her eyes suffered a hemorrhage; and her nose and mouth were bruised. Her hands were bound by shoelaces and were attached to the neck ligature. It was posited that the more the victim struggled, the tighter the ligature became and that the suspect did this repeated times before finally killing her.

There were copious amounts of seminal fluid at the scene on Davis' nightgown and sheets, and vaginal and anal swabs demonstrated the presence of spermatozoa. The amount of semen suggested that the perpetrator repeatedly masturbated while alternatingly tightening and releasing the pressure of the ligature on Davis' neck. Two foreign hairs were found in the victim's pubic hair that were later identified through forensic analysis as being Negroid and, subsequently, consistent with Spencer's underarm hair. With respect to the semen, investigators discovered that the suspect was a secretor, defined as someone whose blood characteristics are found in other bodily fluids such as seminal fluid.

Analysis of Spencer's blood revealed him to be a Type O, enzyme grouping PGM type 1, PGM subtype 1+, peptidase A type 1. This particular configuration is shared by 13 percent of the population; however, specific characteristics of the analyzed DNA demonstrated that the sample would match only one in 705 million Black individuals. There are only approximately ten million adult Black males in the United States.

Dr. Susan Hellams

Two weeks' after Davis' death, on 2 October Spencer struck again when he beat, raped, tortured, and killed Dr. Susan Hellams. Hellams' husband discovered his wife's beaten partially-naked body on the floor of their closet. Point of access was discovered to be a second-story window that had a large portion of screen cut from it. Detective Williams commented that this was one of the most brutal murders he had ever seen.

The medical examiner identified the cause of death as ligature strangulation from two belts around her neck. Hellams also sustained a fractured nose, blunt force injury to her lower lip, a number of bruises and scrapes, and an injury consistent with a shoe on the back of her leg. Petechiae in her eyes suggested that she had been strangled and revived for at least 20 minutes before she was killed which suggested that the assailant was likely aroused by having complete control over his victim, not unlike the Davis case. Evidence of rape and sodomy included seminal fluid on her back and in the gluteal fold; small mucosal tears of the anus; and the presence of spermatozoa on vaginal, rectal, and perianal swabs. Additionally, an ample amount of seminal fluid was found on the victim's skirt and slip. Subsequent forensic and serologic examination determined that the seminal fluid and spermatozoa were consistent with Spencer's secretion type and could not have belonged to Hellams' husband. DNA analysis ultimately proved that the fluids were Spencer's.

After Hellams' murder, the unknown perpetrator was dubbed the "Southside Strangler" and the area went into panic mode over the term "serial killer." Panic ensued in Richmond; residents of the area left their lights on all the time, every deadbolt lock was purchased from stores, and even dogs from local animal shelters were adopted in record amounts. Police had told single women to nail their windows shut. A preliminary profile suggested that he was a white adult male, approximately 35 years old, a loner, intelligent, not a criminal beginner, and likely had considerable success as a cat burglar of sorts due to his agility and ability to enter residences without making a sound.

The police sought to find a connection between the victims to help identify a suspect. Nearby Cloverfield Mall in Chesterfield County proved to be that link. Davis had worked in a bookstore and Hellams had purchased books from her.

Diane Cho

Not long after, on 22 November, 15-year old high school student Diane Cho was bound, raped, and strangled to death. Cho lived less than a mile from the Cloverfield Mall and wanted to go to medical school. She was studying in her bedroom when Spencer entered through her bedroom window and overtook her so quickly that her parents and brother who were in the next room didn't hear a thing the entire time Spencer was assaulting and murdering her.

Spencer had carved the infinity symbol on Cho which, according to experts, signified his taking, keeping, and sealing the victim for himself since she was a virgin.

Cho lived very close to the Cloverfield Mall.

Susan Tucker

While on furlough from the halfway house in Arlington visiting his family for Thanksgiving, Spencer attacked Susan Tucker, 44, in the same fashion as his other victims on or about 27 November (her body wasn't discovered until 1 December). She was home alone at the time as her husband was away on a business trip. Spencer entered through a basement window and Davis was hog-tied with a rope, raped, and subsequently died from ligature strangulation. When her body was found she had been dead for a few days and those on the scene remarked that it was extremely disturbing and unsettling.

During her autopsy four-to-eight intact non-motile sperm were collected from vaginal swabs and DNA from semen stains were determined to have been left by a secretor. As mentioned, Spencer was that secretor.

Carol Hamm

Back on 25 January 1984, 32-year-old attorney Carolyn Hamm was raped, bound, and hanged in the door between her garage and house. Her body was found naked, face down, and her robe was on the living room floor alongside a piece of cord cut from a Venetian blind and a knife.

At the time, a McDonald's janitor, David Vasquez, was arrested and convicted of Hamm's murder after two witnesses placed him on her street that day. Despite police having doubt that Vasquez was guilty because of his less-than-70 IQ, he did confess and was, subsequently, serving a 35-year prison sentence. Authorities wondered if he had a partner who might still be at large.

Absent any leads at the time, Detective Horgas visited Vasquez at the Buckingham Correctional Center near the Blue Ridge Mountains on 7 December 1988. Vasquez seemed confused; he retracted his confession insisting that he couldn't have killed Hamm because he didn't drive and had no way to get to her house after work. He also denied having an accomplice. After the interview Horgas told the warden that he believed Vasquez to be innocent.

Other Crimes

Prior to Hamm's murder, there was a string of rapes between June 1983 and January 1984 in Arlington. Nine women had been attacked by a masked Black male in his 20s who carried a knife and broke into their homes via a window and who was dubbed the "black masked rapist." The last rape, in fact, occurred on the day Hamm's body was discovered. Detective Horgas wondered whether these rapes and Hamm's murder were connected. When he heard about the first two murders in Richmond, Horgas called Detective Williams to discuss the similarities between Horgas' rapes and the Hamm murder in Arlington and the two (at that time) murders in Richmond. Williams also mentioned a recent attack in Davis' and Hellams' neighborhood wherein a Black masked man had entered a woman's apartment through a window and was in the process of tying her up when neighbors came over to investigate noises and scared him away. Whereas Horgas was virtually convinced that the crimes in both Arlington and Richmond had been committed by the same person, Williams was skeptical due to the distance between the two cities and the fact that FBI profilers asserted that serial killers are almost always White.

Williams did tell Horgas that the Richmond police were trying DNA testing which, he said, identified an individual's unique genetic material that is found in every cell of a person's body and that they had already sent samples from the Davis and Hellams murders to Lifecodes, a New York State private laboratory that analyzed DNA for paternity tests. Prior to this, nobody in the United States had ever used DNA testing in a homicide investigation.

The Investigation

All of the murders shared overwhelmingly similar characteristics which demonstrated that the deceased were the victim of a serial killer with a particular signature that was unique to him. All of the victims were bound—wrists to neck—with handmade tourniquets fashioned from materials the killer found at the house through which he could repeatedly tighten and loosen the ligatures so that he could suffocate and revive the victims multiple times. There was substantial semen left at the crime scene near the body which suggested that the suspect likely masturbated while torturing his victims. None of the victims had defensive injuries which demonstrated that they were overcome quickly. All of the victims were White or Asian with a "stocky" build. All of the murders occurred on the weekend. Additionally, in every case the victims' bodies were laid crosswise on their beds (except for Hellams who was in her closet) representing submissiveness and in each case the victims' were "covered": Davis was redressed in shorts, a sheet was placed over Cho's buttocks, a blanket was placed over Tucker's buttocks, and Hellams' closet door was closed. Some experts have suggested that posing the bodies enabled the perpetrator to extend the crime scenes to make him feel even more powerful than he already did and that his covering them was like putting a lid on a trash can. The point of entry in every case was through a window in which glass was either broken or a screen was cut.

Detective Horgas was the first to overcome what is known as "linkage blindness" in which clues exist to link particular crimes but the Richmond investigators wore blinders as to how certain cases were, in fact, linked. One of the most glaring examples of this was that Richmond police were so intent on looking for a White suspect based upon their preliminary profile and, therefore, were initially against considering the possibility that the killer was, in fact, Black.

Horgas also reinterviewed the burglary and rape victims from Arlington prior to Hamm's murder. He discovered glaring similarities and a pattern of escalation that ultimately culminated with the perpetrator "graduating" to murder. Similarities included the fact that the point of entry was always through a window; lengths of Venetian blind cords had been cut and found near the crime scenes in multiple cases; and victims had been tied up, raped, and tortured. In some cases the victims' mouths were covered with duct tape (Cho's mouth was also taped). The fifth victim was locked in a car that was lit on fire but she was able to kick her way out and escape. Perhaps most damning was that the three-year break in between Hamm's death and the other four women's deaths correlated to the time that Spencer was in prison and that for every recent murder he had signed out of the halfway house; even seeking approval for a furlough to return to Arlington for the Thanksgiving holiday.

And then there was the DNA evidence. In addition to the samples from Richmond, Horgas hand-delivered samples from the Hamm and Tucker murders as well as some of the rapes to Lifecodes on 28 December 1988.

While waiting for the results, on 29 December FBI agents Stephen Mardigan and Judson Ray from the Behavioral Science Unit at Quantico went to Arlington to examine Horgas' evidence and ultimately agreed with his theory that the crimes in both cities had been committed by the same person. The profilers said that the key to all of the crimes was to reexamine the first rape in Arlington and that the perpetrator likely lived nearby because he would have wanted to commit his first assault where he felt comfortable such as in his own neighborhood. The agents also iterated that based upon their profile, this type of person would only stop if he were incarcerated of died. This spurred Horgas to look for a suspect who was arrested and incarcerated shortly after Hamm's murder in January 1984 and released just prior to the first Richmond murder in September 1987.

Spencer demonstrated classic signatures of an anger-retaliatory rapist-murderer who utilized sexualized violence against women who are perceived to have threatened or otherwise harmed the killer's self-image. Most of these perpetrators targeted victims usually in the same age range or older than the killer; however, in the case of Cho, despite being only 15 she looked older. Since he cannot kill the actual target of his anger he finds surrogate targets who he stalks prior to the assault. Spencer punished his victims for some wrongdoing by systematically degrading, humiliating, and incapacitating them.

The next day Horgas drove to South Oxford Street where the first victim was assaulted in a nearby wooded lot after being abducted from a phone booth at South Glebe Road and Second Street in June 1983. He racked his brain trying to remember who he may have arrested nearby during that time. He and his partner Mike Hill then went through over 300 files trying to recall. Four days later the name Timmy popped into his head. Horgas remembered investigating Timmy for burglary and arson of either a house or car. On 6 January 1988 Horgas remembered Timmy's last name: Spencer. Horgas conducted a driver's license check for Timothy Spencer and found that he resided in Richmond and that he had been arrested on 29 January 1984 for a burglary in Alexandria, Virginia, just four days after police discovered Hamm's body. After serving time in prison, Spencer was released to a halfway house in the Southside area on 4 September 1987—a mere two weeks before Davis was killed. Further, Spencer's mother lived less than a mile from both murder sites in Arlington and a mere 200 yards from the Oxford Street crime scene. Horgas said that it was like a puzzle wherein all the pieces fit together perfectly. On an interesting side note, had it not been for Horgas' memory he would never have found Spencer's name in any of the parole files through which he looked so diligently as convicts released to halfway houses were not technically considered paroled.

Spencer was placed under surveillance by the Richmond Police Department; however, after a week without him doing anything suspicious the surveillance was called off. This was much to the dismay of Arlington prosecutor Helen Fahey who—not unlike Tucker—was a single woman who lived alone in a rented townhouse far too similar to Tucker's home. She contacted Horgas and the two brainstormed ideas of how to get Spencer off the street before he struck again. Fahey suggested asking for a grand jury indictment which was considerably more difficult to challenge in court that an arrest warrant.

Arrest

On 20 January 1988 at 5:50 p.m. with his grand jury indictment in hand Horgas arrested Spencer at his Richmond halfway house on suspicion of burglary.

During the drive back to Arlington, Spencer was very tight-lipped, not volunteering any statements. Horgas knew that he needed either a confession or Spencer's consent to volunteer a blood sample. Horgas asked Spencer to submit to a blood test under the guise that it was necessary to compare to some blood found on a broken window in a burglary. Unaware of the advent of DNA analysis and that a blood test could be utilized to match a semen sample, Spencer agreed, to the delight and astonishment of Horgas.

On 16 March Horgas was notified that Spencer's DNA matched fluids left at the murders of Davis, Hellams, and Tucker, as well as one of the Arlington rapes four years earlier. Both Horgas and Fahey knew they had just caught a serial killer but Fahey had to convince a jury of Spencer's guilt based upon fledgling scientific evidence that she needed jurors to understand and accept in order to obtain a capital murder conviction. In fact, due to the relative infancy and lack of knowledge about DNA evidence, trial judge Benjamin Kendrick held a special hearing to determine whether the evidence was even legally admissible. After considerable inquiry Kendrick decided that the evidence was credible and would be admitted into trial.

Trials

On 11 July 1988 Spencer went on trial in Arlington for the murder of Susan Tucker. On 16 July after only six hours of jury deliberation, Spencer was found guilty of capital murder and sentenced to death. This was the first case in the United States in which a defendant was found guilty of capital murder and received the death penalty based upon DNA evidence; a noteworthy distinction, indeed.

Spencer's Richmond trials began in the Circuit Court of the City of Richmond, Manchester Courthouse on 17 January 1989 and ultimately, on 22 September 1989, he was found guilty of rape, burglary, sodomy, and capital murder and was unanimously sentenced to death following several unsuccessful appeals of his conviction and death sentence at both state and federal levels. It didn't help his case any that when the jury was shown crime scene photos Spencer was very eager to look at them as well; essentially wanting to revisit the excitement he experienced when he brutalized the victims. Aside from this display of enthusiasm Spencer demonstrated absolutely no remorse or other emotion.

In his first appeal with Supreme Court of Virginia, Spencer raised five issues: that the DNA evidence was unreliable; that his defense team was denied the opportunity to adequately defend against said evidence because the trial court denied a discovery request for Lifecodes' notes and memoranda, that the trial court refused to provide funds for an expert DNA witness for the defense, and that the prosecution failed to reveal any evidence of problems with Lifecodes' testing process; that the trial court wrongly admitted the DNA evidence; that the prosecution improperly removed a juror for alleged racially-motivated reasons in violation of *Batson v. Kentucky*, 476 U.S. 79 (1986); and that the attached aggravating factor of "future dangerousness" is unconstitutionally vague. The Court upheld the lower court's ruling. The United States Supreme Court denied certiorari.

On 10 September 1990 Spencer filed a petition for a writ of habeas corpus with the state trial court which was ultimately dismissed on 15 November that same year and subsequently affirmed by the Supreme Court of Virginia. Next, Spencer filed another habeas corpus petition in the United States District Court for the Eastern District of Virginia which was also denied. He then requested a Certificate of Probable Cause to appeal which was also denied by the United States Court of Appeals, Fourth Circuit. An additional Notice of Appeal and request for Certificates of Probable Cause were filed in district court on 29 April 1993 and 25 May 1993 which were met with the respondent's motion to dismiss. The Fourth Circuit Appellate Court granted Spencer's application for Probable Cause.

In this appeal Spencer's legal team raised seven issues: ineffective assistance of counsel at the original trial because they failed to obtain a defense DNA expert; that he is "actually innocent" of the crimes for which he received the death penalty and would not have been convicted had he been able to challenge the DNA evidence and if the "prejudicial injection of astronomical probability ratios" had not been introduced at trial; that his trial counsel were ineffective due to their failure to conduct voir dire on the subject of racial prejudice; that Virginia's proportionality review is unconstitutional and does not allow "rational exceptions"; that the jury instructions regarding mitigating evidence were constitutionally inadequate; that his trial counsel were ineffective due to their failure to present certain mitigating evidence; and that the DNA analysis was unreliable, should not have been admitted, and, thus, his trial counsel were ineffective with respect to this evidence.

The Fourth Circuit considered some of Spencer's issues. First, with respect to ineffective assistance of counsel, the court turned to *Strickland v. Washington*, 466 U.S. 668 (1984), in which the United States Supreme Court stated that in order to prevail on an ineffective assistance of counsel claim the petitioner must demonstrate that not only did counsel perform deficiently but that the petitioner suffered prejudice as a result. Both factors must be present and the burden of proof rests with the petitioner to prove whether there was a reasonable probability that if it were not for counsel's alleged errors the result of the trial would have been different and whether there was a reasonable probability that the sentence would have concluded that other mitigating evidence would not warrant death.

Spencer's claim of ineffective assistance of counsel because of their failure to provide a defense DNA expert was dismissed due to evidence that the court not only discussed with Spencer's counsel about procuring an expert but that because no experts interviewed were willing to testify on the defense's behalf does not make his counsel ineffective. Further, his attorneys had a blind DNA test run by an independent laboratory which corroborated the evidence against Spencer.

As to the voir dire allegation of racial bias, because of the publicity surrounding Spencer's first trial in Richmond, a change of venire—wherein a jury is selected and brought in from another county due to the fear that pretrial publicity would prevent the empaneling of an impartial jury—was granted and the jury was from Norfolk. The Court held that the change of venire eliminated race as an issue with which to be concerned and that it had no reason to believe that any prospective juror had any racial bias against Spencer and this allegation was also dismissed.

With respect to the mitigating evidence concerns, Spencer contended that had his counsel adequately investigated his background that they would have discovered that his school history, presentence report, and Department of Corrections reports all stated that he was troubled; that he was emotionally damaged by being erroneously told that his father was dead when, in fact, he was not; that he regularly ingested PCP; and that he may have some degree of organic brain damage and that his counsel failed to appoint a psychologist to evaluate his mental state. The Court said that the record reflected that Spencer's counsel did, in fact, conduct a thorough background investigation which yielded evidence that Spencer's attorneys in the Arlington trial had hired both a psychiatrist and psychologist who mutually found a complete lack of any mitigating circumstances and ceased any more investigation because of fear that more incriminating evidence might have been uncovered. In fact, per the recommendation of the Richmond criminal defense bar, Dr. Robert Mullaney conducted a pretrial evaluation of Spencer and Spencer's attorneys decided to not utilize Dr. Mullaney as a witness because the sole "plus"—Mullaney's opinion that Spencer's future dangerousness would be minimized if kept in prison—was far outweighed by the potential negatives which would ensue had Dr. Mullaney testified: these being the jury finding out that Spencer committed the offense, denied his guilt, and had shown no remorse whatsoever. Further, the defense counsel stated that if they had used Dr. Mullaney then the prosecution would have been entitled to have Spencer evaluated by its own expert.

As for Spencer's claim of defense counsel's deficiency in handling adequately DNA evidence, the Court argued that his counsel did, in fact, conduct a thorough investigation and contacted several experts, some of whom assisted throughout the trial but were unwilling to testify and, therefore, determined that counsel was not ineffective simply because they could not find an expert willing to testify. Further, regarding his "actual innocence" claim and that he would not have been convicted if the "prejudicial injection of astronomical probability ratios" into the trial record had not occurred, because a claim of "actual innocence" is not a constitutional claim then—and differs from a claim of "factual innocence"— the Court's discretion was limited. Ultimately, the Court held that Spencer failed to demonstrate any constitutional error that could have affected the jury's verdict. Further, the trial judge heard all of the information regarding DNA analysis including its statistics and limitations and still decided to admit the evidence into court.

Spencer's execution date was set for 26 August 1993.

Execution

Desperate last-minute appeals for a stay of execution were denied by the United States Supreme Court and Timothy Wilson Spencer was executed on 27 April 1994. He was pronounced dead at 11:13 p.m. He was 32 at the time of his death.

Virginia author and veteran detective Lee Lofland attended Spencer's execution and described, on his website, the atmosphere at the prison as "nothing short of surreal." He stated that Spencer entered on his own, calmly took a seat in the chair, and permitted the "death squad" to secure him and attach electrodes. His face was completely devoid of any sign of fear, regret, or sadness. When asked whether Spencer had any final words it appeared that he might say something but then stopped, silently. Lofland described how Spencer made eye contact with him and even made a two-thumbs-up gesture until the leather mask was placed over his head and he was executed.

On execution day, Davis' friend Lorna Wyckoff called Spencer a "monster" and the "personification of evil." Spencer's brother Travis said it was the most difficult day of his life, hugging his brother for the last time.

Post-Execution

Whereas DNA evidence proved critical for finding Spencer guilty, it was far more difficult procuring David Vasquez's exoneration since the samples from the Hamm murder were too degraded. Vasquez would need a pardon from the governor. Fahey formerly requested the assistance of FBI Special Agent John Douglas who had founded the Behavioral Science Unit in the early 1980s after interviewing some of the most notorious serial killers in history such as Ted Bundy, Charles Manson, and David Berkowitz, and identifying patterns in their behavior; their unique "signatures." Douglas' agreement to assist was the first time FBI profilers had ever been asked to prove a suspect's innocence.

Douglas said that one must look for a signature to link similar cases and that a signature was a type of ritual performed by a suspect that is truly unique. Douglas believed that the nature of how Spencer bound his victims constituted a distinctive signature in the five homicides and that use of ligatures and ropes exceeded the necessary amount of force necessary to control the victims was also part of his signature. On 4 January 1989 Vasquez was pardoned and became the first person exonerated, albeit indirectly, by DNA evidence.

Spencer's conviction was such a landmark case because it broadened the public and professional knowledge about DNA and that the jury understood its significance and was able to convict a serial killer of capital murder was a major revelation. The case also prompted Virginia to open the first state DNA laboratory in the United States in 1989 and to set up the first DNA database.

Shortly thereafter, in 1992, the Innocence Project came into being. A nonprofit founded by New York's Benjamin Cardozo School of Law, the Innocence Project has worked to free 179 of the 337 people exonerated by DNA evidence, including 20 who were on death row. The most common reason cited for wrongful convictions is erroneous eyewitness identification with mishandling of forensic evidence due to faulty tests and/or procedural errors the second reason. DNA is not completely infallible, however. The Innocence Project states that approximately four percent of those exonerated were originally convicted as a result of improperly conducted DNA tests which have prompted virtually all defense attorneys in criminal proceedings to request retesting on their clients' behalf.

In addition to Paul Mones' (1995) book *Stalking Justice: The Dramatic True Story of the Detective Who First Used DNA Testing to Catch a Serial Killer* that focused upon Detective Horgas' efforts to link his cases in Arlington to those in Richmond and, ultimately, to

Spencer, Spencer's case provided the basis for Patricia Cornwell's first crime novel *Postmortem* (1990) as she, at the time was employed as a computer analyst in the Richmond, Virginia's Office of the Chief Medical Examiner. Former FBI profiler John Douglas devoted chapter 11 of his 1996 memoir *Journey into Darkness* to Spencer. His case also inspired the forensic science documentary *Medical Detectives* which first aired on 31 October 1996.

CANNIBAL : THE TRUE STORY OF KARL DENKE

145

NATHAN HAYES

Karl Denke: A Real-Life Psychopath

Karl Denke is perhaps the most twisted, disturbed man of the last 200 years. This is a man who was much more than a killer. This is a man who not only murdered over 40 people in the early 1900's, but also cannibalized them for himself and unsuspecting people. The stories of Karl Denke are beyond human comprehension; the details are simply too gruesome to understand. Karl Denke is arguably the most evil man that many have never heard of.

The life of Karl Denke is one that is largely unknown. Even his gruesome crimes and psychotic, murderous years are little known to the general public. At a time that the world was in the midst of World War I, Denke was waging his own war on unsuspecting victims in a largely contested area of Europe. Understanding his motives is simply impossible. Perhaps the worst part of the entire life of Karl Denke is the fact that he hanged himself in his jail cell before answers or justice could ever be had. Karl Denke will forever be known as one of the most twisted, disturbing human beings to ever walk the face of the Earth.

Karl Denke had a rather insignificant childhood in the fact that nothing at all special took place. Typically, cases like Karl Denke's can be traced back to traumatic experiences from childhood. That is just not the case with Denke.

Karl Denke was born in 1870 in present-day Kalinowice Gorne which is in lower Salasia. This is a largely urban area of Poland. In 1870, this was an area of vast battle for territory and political desire. Ten years later, Karl Denke was moved to Muensterberg. Muensterberg is present-day Ziebice, Poland. This is a small area of Poland known for agricultural living and urban culture. He was an extremely dull child who largely lacked personality beyond basic function. The style of living is important for his childhood in the sense that he had little opportunity to develop strong social skills.

At the age of 12, Karl Denke dropped out of school to begin working. He became an apprentice to a gardener at this time in Ziebice,

Poland. He held this job for over ten years. He had little incident and seemed to fit right in with what many young workers were at the time. He was on his way to success. At age 25, Denke's father passed away. His brother was given the family farm at this time. Karl was given a significant amount of money to purchase land in Poland to start a farm of his own. For several years, Karl tried to develop a successful farm that would lend solid profits. However, he had little experience in farming and even less desire to lead that style of life.

Karl Denke sold his farm and purchased a home in town on present-day Stawowa Street in Ziebice, Poland. Hard economic times would soon hit the entire region. A recession that rocked all of Europe would leave Karl Denke extremely vulnerable to financial hardship. Like so many other people in this era, Karl was forced to sell this property and move into a small apartment in the same town. The apartment was a one-bedroom on the first floor that famously had a small shed in the backyard. Karl Denke had hit rock bottom, but he had made it through.

In the later years of his life, Karl Denke operated a room and board home in his hometown. He affectionately did this from 1918 to 1924. He was extremely well liked by his tenants. He was commonly called "papa" by those who had been around him at this location for an extended time. For the community as a whole, Karl was very well liked and came off as very mild mannered. Ironically enough, he was even the organ player for the local church. The activities he was taking part in during this time were completely unknown to everyone around him. To everyone, he was the polite older gentlemen that they had the privilege of being around each Sunday at church. He was a great landlord who took care of his tenants in a variety of ways. The truth behind Karl Denke was completely unimaginable to everyone who around him.

The Event that Changed Everything

On December 21, 1924, Karl Denke would meet his death. The events of this day are tragic on many levels. These events also open the book on the secret life of Karl Denke. This is the day that the story of Karl Denke is all uncovered.

It was around 1 P.M. on December 21st that a man barged into the local police station in Ziebice, Poland. The man was covered in blood. It was apparent that he had been in a struggle for his life. He was shaken and stumbling on his words. He seemed to be holding on to a deep fear of whatever had happened to him. This man's name was Vincenz Oliver.

Oliver was a local vagabond. He had frequent yet minor run-ins with the law. Being as the town's population was just under 9,000, seemingly everyone knew each other. Police immediately suspected that Oliver had simply had a typical run in with the wrong crowd. What Vincenz Oliver would tell police would quickly grab their attention, however.

Oliver claimed that Karl Denke had tried to kill him with a pickaxe. Upon examination of his wounds, this seemed to match exactly with the lacerations on his body. A doctor was called in to examine his wounds further. It was confirmed by this doctor that his wounds were likely blunt force trauma lacerations. He also concluded that a pickaxe was a suitable weapon to make the kind of wounds that were present on Oliver's body. Police were utterly shocked that Oliver had named Karl Denke as the suspect. Karl Denke had a great reputation in the community. Even though they presumed that Karl Denke was likely innocent of any wrongdoing, they sought him out to question him on the accident.

Karl Denke was arrested in the late afternoon on December 21, 1924. Denke immediately confirmed that he had attacked Vincenz Oliver with a pickaxe. He explained to police that he was simply defending his property against a burglar. Police initially thought the alibi was valid. While it seemed suspicious that Denke would keep pursuing such an attack after the burglar tried to flee, they still felt like it was a reasonable explanation for the attack. Police decided to hold Karl Denke in custody while an investigation ensued.

The investigation would never see trial, however. Karl Denke hanged himself in his jail cell merely two hours after he was put in. He used his customary handkerchief to do the deed. He was found tied to the cell door by his neck. He died of asphyxiation as a result of hanging. Karl Denke has ended his own life less than 12 hours after committing a random crime against a local small time crook. His own inflicted death happened just two hours after being put into his cell. It was clear to investigators that Karl Denke was hiding something. It was their job, now, to determine what exactly that was.

A Gruesome Discovery

On December 24, 1924, police obtained a warrant to search Karl Denke's home. What the team would find is simply disgusting. In one of the most famous investigative reports in recent history, Friedrich Pietrusky documented the findings in the home of Karl Denke. Below is the official investigative report of the scene.

"The first findings made in Denke's house during the search were bones and pieces of meat. The latter were in a salt solution found in a wooden drum. There were altogether 15 pieces of meat with the skin. Two parts of the breast, which is strongly hairy. The torso is cut through the middle, three fingers above the navel. Its lateral limit is the front shoulder blade. In the piece of the anterior abdominal wall, the middle of the navel is visible. The remaining pieces belong to the side and back parts. The largest is about 40 by 20 centimeters large. Particularly striking was a very clean anus with hand large parts of both buttocks."

"The meat is brownish red and does not feel as if the body would have lost much blood. On the back some soft-bluish discoloration is visible as well as livor mortis, which leads to the conclusion that the disassembly of the body took place several hours after death."

"There is no evidence of vital reaction of the bodies to the cuts made, which means that the latter were not made while the victims were still alive. Nevertheless, some skin and muscles from the necks were missing, as well as extremities (arms and legs), head, and sexual organs. Lesions could not be determined, nor the nature of death of the tool or weapon of the crime."

"In three medium-sized pots filled with cream sauce, some cooked meat, partially covered with skin and human hair was found. The meat was pink and very soft. All pieces seemed cut off from the gluteal area. (Buttocks) One pot had only half of a portion. Denke must have eaten the other piece shortly before being arrested."

This account is a famous writing from the crime scene that details only a small portion of the findings. Each of these statement is pure fact. The last sentence regarding Denke is pure assumption however, based off of the findings at the scene. The portion was visibly gone, however it was impossible to prove or disprove that it was Karl Denke who had eaten it.

Karl Denke clearly had many skeletons in his closet, most literally. It was clear to investigators that he had killed all of these victims and dismembered them after the fact. It was also clear that much of the meat was gone. It is widely believed that Denke sold the meat at local gatherings. It is speculated that he even gave the human meat to guests that he would have over in his home. This is pure speculation however.

Pietrusky also points out some of the obvious problems with establishing what specifically happened to the meat.

"I should like to mention here that there is no evidence that Denke has ever sold the meat of his victims. All of the evidence, however, has been eaten. However, it seems certain that his guest, the vagabonds, were offered to eat it."

Could this have been the motive behind the attack on Vincenz Oliver? It most definitely appears to be the reason. Oliver knew Denke well. Vincenz knew Karl Denke well enough to voluntarily enter his home. He obviously trusted Karl and didn't know the truth behind what was going on.

Pietrusky goes on to document further. Again, each revelation that is written by Pietrusky seems to escalate in severity. The disgusting nature of the home of Karl Denke is mind-blowing.

"In the third pot, numerous pieces of human skin and parts of aorta in a gelatinous mass. A bowl on his table in his room was filled with amber colored fat, of which appeared to be human. Biological test gave a positive result for human protein."

"In the shed, in which the meat pieces were found, was also a barrel full of bones that were cleaned of tendons, muscles, etc. that most probably have been cooked prior. The investigation initially revealed the existence of six forearm bones, which means that they belonged to three people at least. More traces were found behind the shed. A part of a leg remained in the pond that Denke had dug many years before and also skeletal pieces were uncovered in the local forest. Here is a full list of what has been sent to us for examination from the forest:

-Sixteen femurs of which one pair of remarkably strong ones, two pairs of very thin ones, six pairs and two left femurs.

-Fifteen medium-sized pieces of long bones.

-Four pairs of elbow bones.

-Seven heads of radii.

-Nine lower parts of radii.

-Eight lower parts of elbow.

-A pair of upper shinbone.

-A pair of lower elbows and radii, of which extremities still remained connected.

-A pair of upper arms as well as upper arm heads.

-A pair of collar bones.

-Two shoulder blades.

-Eight heels and ankle bones.

-One hundred and twenty toes and phalanx.

-Sixty-five feet and metacarpal bones.

-Five first ribs and one hundred-fifty pieces of ribs.

"All of the bones, with the exception of only a very few, were fatless, very light, and very porous. In the forest also remained parts of a spine and clean parts of a male dissected pelvis. The pelvis showed extreme evidence of saw-cutting. Only one piece of head bone was found. This was a piece of the inferior petrosal sinus area, very jagged on the front side. It looks broken and bears considerable signs of sharp sawing on its top. This piece of bone had been cross marked with a dark ink."

"Given the size and the condition of the bones, we can assume, that there was one very strong individual and two others were of delicate bone structure."

"The cutting surfaces of the bones are very jagged, as if blunt force was applied, such as the blunt end of an axe or a hammer. Some of the bones were visibly sawed. Few spots show traces of a sharp, well maintained tool. This is most likely axe strikes. Similarly, such traces were found on the articulations, which must have been cut out with a knife."

"Based on the findings that we uncovered and upon deep examination of all of the evidence, we were able to come to the conclusion that the forest held the remains of at least eight individuals."

To put this all in perspective, the human bone collection were the initial uncovering of just the forest near the home. This doesn't take in to account the bodies of the individuals in the home or the shed. This was also just the initial findings. In the years after the initial investigation, many more bones would be discovered. In fact, the last discovery of bones from the Karl Denke case were made in the late 1940's, just after the end of WWII. The overall scope of this case is mind-blowing. Even more disturbing still was the further explanation of the investigation lead by Pietrusky.

"Considerably more revealing was Denke's dental collection. We received a total of 351 teeth from both the forest and the home of Karl Denke."

"These were found in a moneybag and in two tin boxes, on which "pepper" and "salt" was written, as well as in three paper bags, which were destined to keep pepper. They were partly sorted according to their size: the molars were in the moneybag, while the others were in the two boxes and in the paper bag. In yet another paper bag were teeth that most likely belonged to a single person, and in a third bag three lower incisors were found with strongly atrophic structure. This one likely came from an old individual. All of the teeth, with the exception of only six, were very well preserved."

The overall results the Pietrusky's team were able to conclude are staggering. He goes on to account a "final tally" of the evidence and the conclusions based off of these findings. Interestingly enough, the numbers of the victims are unknown; they can only be put to a bare minimum due to incompleteness of so many bodies. Likely, the sheer number of victims will never officially be known. It is widely agreed by several other investigations since the Pietrusky investigation that the number is much higher than has been concluded.

"The investigation led us to many important details. The remains of the bones were most definitely a minimum of eight victims, however other circumstances of the case make it likely that the overall number of victims is much higher. The teeth that were found belonged most certainly to at least twenty people. Professor Euler noted that some individual teeth appear more than twice as often as is statistically expected. This suggests that the number of victims could be even higher than expected."

"The fact that the majority of the victims suffered from caries leads us to think that the number of victims was higher. In addition, it must be stated that people in old age lacked proper dental treatment.

Professor Euler estimates cautiously that the teeth belonged to at least twenty-five different individuals."

"The extractions were done in many different ways. Some teeth seem to have been taken out quite easily due to senile atrophy, while others were rather solidly rooted and extracted with force. In several cases we discerned parts of the alveolar wand. Some specimens, especially the molars and premolars show fractures in tooth enamel that couldn't have occurred during the victim's lifetime. On some, there are traces of claws with very sharp edges. The appearance of some roots seems to justify the assumption that the jaw had been cooked in advance of the extraction. Again, Denke had no luck."

Further details of the investigation are especially odd. Typically, crimes of a similar magnitude have some sort of trend or significance to the killer. It may be the sex of the victim or the age in some instances. The investigation, using the best methods available at the time, yielded no true trend to the victims. This is not at all common to mass murder cases.

"Especially interesting is the answer to the question of the age of the victims. From the list later mentioned we know nearly all of the victims. There are no young victims among them. Now, there are four wisdom teeth that clearly came from the same individual that have peculiarities usually found on the teeth of the fifty year old. The investigation of the other teeth showed that at least four-fifths of the victims were seniors. Professor Euler summarized that among the victims there was certainly one person who was not any older than sixteen years old. The majority, however, were significantly older than fifty years old. Two individuals were probably between twenty and thirty years old and another that was likely between thirty and forty years old."

"The tests did not give satisfactory results concerning the sex of the individuals, nor their jobs. For obvious reasons, nothing specific can be said about the time that elapsed after their death. What is certain is only that some teeth had been extracted many years ago. The pulling of the tooth of a young person must have taken place weeks ago. In any case, the study of the teeth brought much more information regarding the number and age of the victims than could be learned by just the bones, but it must be taken into consideration that the latter were only partially recovered."

The next part of the account of the investigation is equally chilling. The investigation team delved into greater depths into the personal belongings of Karl Denke. The discoveries made show that Denke kept maintained records of his victims, and possibly the date of which he killed them.

"Among Denke's suspenders were three pair of human skin suspenders. They were roughly six centimeters wide and seventy or so centimeters long. The leather is not at all smooth and at one spot was broken. It seems as to not be tanned, but only free of sub-skin tissue and dried. At one spot it is quite obvious that he made cuts just under the nipples, which are still clearly visible. Four are patched with human skin taken from the pubic area. There are some traces of louse nits that were discerned under a microscope. All suspenders show traces of use and one of them was found on Denke himself."

"Besides the suspenders, Denke also had leather straps cut out of human skin, that he treated with shoe polish and parts of which were sewn together with pieces of cloth. Many of these laces were made with human hair; one sample was just one centimeter long, grey-white and, according to the study, taken from the human head."

"Equally strange was Denke's collection of coins. This consists of round, flat unfired clay pieces, size ranging from a Pfennig to fifty Pfennigs, which have just one side of the image of the coin."

"A large number of ID cards and personal papers of several different people were found in Denke's room as well as account books on revenue from the garden, on working hours and so on. They were relatively well managed and clear. More attention was attached to some loose sheets of paper on which names of thirty men and women appear. In front of every name is a date, probably the date of death of the person. At number 31 is only a date. The record is perfectly chronological. Numbering starts at number eleven. In case of women, only the first name is indicated. The notes for men are much more detailed and thorough, usually with a date of birth, place of stay, and the status of the person concerned. The assumption that this is the list of victims justified by the fact that, ID cards found in Denke's room, belonged to people whose whereabouts could not otherwise be identified. By the appearance of the sheets, we can assume, that the list had not been made in one day."

"On one side of the sheets are the initials of the name followed by a number, which most likely indicated the weight of the person concerned. On another slip of paper, next to a name stands what follows: 'dead, 122, naked, 107, disemboweled, 83'. This last figure is then repeated next to the name of the person concerned in the last table."

"Of the tools used for the killings and fragmentation of the bodies, these can be said:
-Three axes.
-A large wood saw.
-A tree saw
-A pickaxe
-Three knives.

"All of these have been seized by us with the exception of the axes and the tree saw, which are sent to be tested for traces of human blood and tissue. The saw is a large tool, with which, as the microscopic examination revealed, also had wood particles on it. The detection of human blood succeeded. However, we suppose that he used much finer tools, probably the tree saw, to cut heads and pelvic bones. The pickaxe was used for the last assassination attempt and human blood can be stated on this tool as well. It has a length of forty centimeters and is pointed forward. As for the knives, we could not make things all clear."

With this full report, it has left open one major question over all of these years: How could Karl Denke have committed such heinous crimes for over fifteen years and never been caught?

Apparently, the signs of something being off with Karl Denke were noticeable. While Vincenz Oliver escaped an assassination attempt at the hands of Denke, two other men accomplished the same thing in the decade before. For unknown reasons, however, they never came forward to police to report the crime.

The first instance was with an apprentice to Denke whom escaped the house while covered in blood. Shortly after, he disappeared and was never heard from again. Instead of reporting to police upon his escape, he hesitated, and presumably became a victim at a later time.

The second incident was a vagabond who was asked to write a letter for Denke. He soon found himself with a chain around his neck. He was much stronger than Denke and managed to escape with his life. Ironically enough, this man informed the neighbors of what had happened. This was never reported to police until after Denke's death.

The story of Karl Denke can't be summed up with just a few short words to try find a reasoning behind his behavior. Crimes such as the Denke Murder's just don't happen. The true number of victims at the hands of Karl Denke will most certainly never be known. The true scope of violence that this man portrayed can't be exaggerated. Karl Denke was one of the most twisted human beings to walk the Earth.

www.ingramcontent.com/pod-product-compliance
Lightning Source LLC
Chambersburg PA
CBHW021452150726

47989CB00001B/501